BOWL STORIES

BEN DONATH
& VIOLA MOLZEN

teNeues

CONTENTS

AS OUR TRAIN TRIP FROM BERLIN TO MUNICH WAS DRAWING TO A CLOSE, A FELLOW PASSENGER ASKED US HOW WE WERE ABLE TO TALK ABOUT FOOD FOR SEVEN HOURS STRAIGHT. WE LAUGHED AND ANSWERED, "BECAUSE WE LOVE FOOD!"

Our names are Viola Molzen and Benjamin Donath. As residents of Berlin by choice, we discovered that we share childhood memories as well as the desire to search for new flavor experiences—and sometimes both at the same time. Because we cook for meat lovers and vegetarians, for people with food allergies and for vegans, we have labeled all the dishes in this book accordingly. In the end, however, the sky is the limit as far as imagination goes: It's a snap to make a vegetarian dish vegan, and it's just as easy to add fish or meat to anything you like. The main thing is that you end up with something delicious and surprising on your plate.

With *Bowl Stories*, however, nothing goes on a plate—instead, everything is served in a bowl. Rather than following a trend, this cookbook expresses our love for food itself. A bowl can be easily cradled in one hand and carried everywhere. Instead of eating at the table, you can sit on the couch and eat while watching your favorite movie, celebrate breakfast in bed, or eat at the windowsill and simply let your thoughts drift as you gaze into the distance. Unlike *Abundance Bowls*, which focus on clean eating and superfoods, we define our bowl recipes as the ultimate comfort food. We include ingredients that blend beautifully on a spoon but can just as easily stand on their own. Eating from a bowl is about combining and standing apart, and it is about all the associated rituals: the spoon that scrapes the inside rim of the bowl for the last time, or sharing food from a large pot with your best friend. And especially that moment when you hold the bowl in one hand while the other hand guides the spoon to your mouth for the first bite and you close your eyes to savor the flavors—that is the epitome of taking it slow.

In our book we present bowl stories for individuals and large families, for quiet and loud moments, for festive occasions and everyday meals. These are recipes for everyone who enjoys cooking and likes to experiment, as well as those who appreciate the traditional yet are open to new ideas. We share with you dishes designed to feed the soul. There is only one rule: In the end, everything has to fit into a bowl.

VIOLA & BEN

WE HAVE USED THE FOLLOWING SYMBOLS TO MARK OUR RECIPES:

 GLUTEN-FREE   **VEGETARIAN**

 LACTOSE-FREE   **VEGAN**

SAVORY
BOWLS

SURF & TURF MEATBALLS IN CAPER CREAM SAUCE

SERVES 2

INGREDIENTS

Meatballs
1 shallot
3 tbsp jarred capers
2 jarred anchovy fillets
1 tbsp butter
2 tbsp milk
1 oz/30 g white bread, cut into cubes
½ lb/250 g ground veal
1 tsp mustard
1 tsp minced chives
1 medium egg
Salt, pepper, sugar
Red pepper flakes

Prawns and sauce
2 tbsp butter
3 tbsp all-purpose flour
2 tbsp heavy cream
3 tbsp jarred capers
Salt, pepper, sugar
2 sprigs tarragon
4 prawns or jumbo shrimp
Vegetable oil
1 tsp vermouth

To serve
2 caperberries, halved
Chives

PREPARATION

Meatballs

1. Peel the shallot, then finely dice it with the capers and anchovies. Heat the butter in a saucepan and sauté the shallot mixture. Add the milk and the cubed bread and stir.

2. Combine the shallot-bread mixture, ground veal, mustard, chives, and egg and season with salt, pepper, sugar, and pepper flakes to taste.

3. In a saucepan, bring 2 cups/500 ml of salted water to a boil, then remove from the heat. Form the meat mixture into 1-inch/2.5-cm balls, place in the simmering water, and steep for about 5 minutes.

Prawns and sauce

1. Heat 1 tablespoon of the butter in a saucepan and brown the flour in the butter. Gradually stir in the water you cooked the meatballs in. Add the cream, capers, and some of the caper liquid. Season the sauce with salt, pepper, and sugar to taste and add the meatballs to the pot.

2. Wash the tarragon and spin dry. Rinse the prawns in cold water and pat dry. Heat some oil in a skillet and briefly stir-fry the prawns on both sides. Add the rest of the butter and the tarragon. Deglaze the pan with the vermouth and season with salt.

TO SERVE

Arrange the meatballs and sauce in two bowls and add two prawns to each bowl. Decorate with halved caperberries and some chives.

Bowl: Royal Copenhagen

KALE

SERVES 2

INGREDIENTS

Onion
½ red onion
2 tbsp apple cider vinegar
2 bay leaves
5 allspice berries
Salt, sugar

Kale
3½ oz/100 g kale
3½ oz/100 g cauliflower
Vegetable oil
2 tsp unsalted butter
1 tsp tahini (sesame paste)
½ tsp curry powder
Red pepper flakes
Salt, pepper, sugar

For serving
Toasted sesame seeds
3 oz/80 g blue cheese

PREPARATION

Onion
1. Peel the onion and cut into wedges.

2. In a saucepan, bring ¼ cup/60 ml water to a boil along with the vinegar, bay leaves, allspice berries, and salt and sugar to taste. Add the onion wedges, cover, and simmer over low heat for 5 minutes.

Kale
1. Wash the kale and the cauliflower, then cut the cauliflower into small florets. Heat some oil in a skillet, then brown the cauliflower florets.

2. Add the butter, tahini, curry powder, and pepper flakes to taste and then season the cauliflower with salt, pepper, and sugar. Remove from the heat.

3. In a saucepan, bring water to a boil with some salt and sugar. Blanch the stemmed kale in the boiling water for 30 seconds. Remove and briefly toss in the pan with the cauliflower.

TO SERVE

Arrange the cauliflower, kale, and onion wedges in two bowls. Sprinkle with sesame seeds and crumble the blue cheese over the top.

VEAL TARTARE
& MARINATED EGG YOLK

SERVES 2

INGREDIENTS

Marinated egg yolk
5 sprigs fresh cilantro
5 chives
½ cup/100 g sugar
2 tbsp salt
2 medium egg yolks

Tartare
2 tbsp coconut palm sugar
2 tbsp soy sauce
1 tsp lime juice
1 tsp miso
3 tbsp apple juice
2 tsp sake (Japanese rice wine)
2 tbsp sesame seeds
2 slices sourdough bread
6 oz/170 g veal (from the round or loin)
8 sprigs fresh cilantro
10 chives

For serving
Chives

Other
Blender (such as a Vitamix Pro 750)
2 serving rings (3 in/8 cm in diameter)

PREPARATION

Marinated egg yolk
1. For the marinade, wash the cilantro and chives and spin dry. Finely puree the herbs with sugar and salt in the blender. Pour enough of the marinade into a bowl to cover the bottom.

2. Place the yolks on the marinade. Carefully cover the yolks with the remaining marinade and refrigerate for 4 hours. Then carefully pour off the marinade.

Tartare
1. Combine the coconut palm sugar, soy sauce, lime juice, miso, apple juice, sake, and sesame seeds in a saucepan and bring to a boil. Simmer for 5 minutes over low heat until reduced. Then chill.

2. Toast the bread and cut out two circles with the serving rings.

3. Cut the veal into small cubes. Wash the cilantro and chives, spin dry, and finely chop separately.

4. Combine the cilantro and marinade with the cubed veal. Lightly press the tartare onto the bread in the serving rings. Sprinkle with chives.

TO SERVE

Place the rings with the tartare in two bowls and remove the rings. Arrange one marinated yolk on each tartare round and decorate with a couple of whole chives.

BOWL WITH WHEAT BERRIES & TARRAGON CROUTONS

SERVES 3

INGREDIENTS

Croutons
2 sprigs tarragon
3 oz/80 g brioche bread or yeast rolls
4 tsp vegetable oil
4 tsp unsalted butter
Salt

Wheat berries
Salt
½ cup/125 g wheat berries,
  soaked overnight
2 oz/50 g kohlrabi
2 oz/50 g broccoli
1½ oz/40 g cauliflower
Olive oil
1 oz/25 g snow peas
2 oz/60 g zucchini
2 sprigs tarragon
⅓ cup/50 g frozen peas
1 tbsp apple cider vinegar
Grated zest from ¼ organic lemon
Pepper, sugar

For serving
¼ cup/10 g baby spinach
2 sprigs tarragon

PREPARATION

Croutons
1. Wash the tarragon and shake dry. Pull apart the brioche into small chunks.

2. Heat the oil in a skillet and toast the brioche chunks until golden. Add the butter and tarragon sprigs and gently toss until the butter foams up. Drain the croutons on paper towels and lightly salt.

Wheat berries
1. Drain and rinse the wheat berries with water. Then cook them in boiling salted water for about 10 minutes. Pour into a sieve and drain. Wash, peel, and trim the vegetables as needed, then cut into bite-size pieces. Wash the tarragon, shake dry, and remove the stems.

2. Heat some oil in a skillet and sauté the vegetables and the peas. Add the vinegar, then season with the tarragon leaves, lemon zest, and salt, pepper, and sugar to taste. Add the wheat berries and lightly toss to combine.

TO SERVE

Wash and shake dry the spinach and tarragon, then remove the leaves from the tarragon. Arrange the wheat berries and the croutons in three bowls and garnish with spinach and tarragon leaves.

Bowl: studio1.berlin

HOKKAIDO LASAGNA

SERVES 2

INGREDIENTS

14 oz/400 g Hokkaido squash
3 tbsp unsalted butter
Grated zest from ¼ organic orange
Salt, pepper, sugar
Grated nutmeg
2½ tbsp crème fraîche
3 tbsp orange juice
1 oz/30 g baby spinach
1 tbsp dried cranberries
4 lasagna noodles

For serving
1 tbsp pumpkin seed oil
Salt
2 tbsp pumpkin seeds
1 handful baby spinach

Other
Blender (such as a Vitamix Pro 750)

PREPARATION

1. Peel the squash and remove the seeds. Cut 5 oz/150 g of the Hokkaido squash into 1-inch/2.5-cm triangular chunks and set aside.

2. Coarsely chop the remaining squash and sauté in a saucepan in half of the butter. Pour in 9 tablespoons of water; season with the orange zest and salt, pepper, sugar, and nutmeg to taste; and cook until tender.

3. Combine the cooked squash and crème fraîche in the blender and puree until smooth. Taste again and adjust the seasonings as needed.

4. Sauté the squash chunks in the remaining butter. Pour in the orange juice, cover, and cook over low heat. Season with salt, pepper, and sugar to taste. Wash the spinach, shake it dry, and together with the cranberries stir into the pumpkin mixture.

5. While the squash is cooking, cook the lasagna noodles in boiling salted water according to the package directions. Remove, drain, and cut in half crosswise.

TO SERVE

Heat the pumpkin seed oil and a pinch of salt in a skillet, add the pumpkin seeds, and toast. Wash the spinach and shake it dry. Spoon some squash puree into two bowls, top with a few chunks of squash, and cover with one of the pieces of lasagna noodle. Continue to layer in this manner until you use up the squash puree, squash triangles, and lasagna noodles. Garnish with pumpkin seeds and spinach.

Bowl: ASA

BEET RISOTTO

SERVES 2

INGREDIENTS

6 oz/170 g beets
4 tsp apple cider vinegar
Salt, pepper, sugar
1 shallot
2½ tbsp butter
½ cup/100 g arborio rice
2½ tbsp white wine
¼ orange
2 tbsp grated Parmesan

For serving
1½ oz/50 g blue cheese
3 tbsp walnuts

PREPARATION

1. Peel the beets, then thinly slice 1 oz/30 g of them. Marinate the slices with the vinegar and salt, pepper, and sugar to taste and set aside until ready to serve.

2. Dice the remaining beets into ¼-inch/5-mm cubes. Peel and chop the shallot.

3. Melt 4 teaspoons of the butter in a saucepan and sauté the shallot. Add the rice and then the wine. Stir in the diced beets and pour in enough hot water to cover the rice.

4. Cook the rice over medium heat, constantly stirring and adding water as needed until the rice is done.

5. Peel and coarsely chop the orange. Stir the orange, Parmesan, and remaining butter into the risotto. Season with salt, pepper, and sugar to taste.

TO SERVE

Crumble the blue cheese into large pieces and coarsely chop the walnuts. Spoon the risotto into two bowls and sprinkle the blue cheese and walnuts over the top. Garnish the risotto with twisted slices of marinated beet.

BELUGA LENTIL SALAD
& SOURDOUGH BREAD

SERVES 2

INGREDIENTS

Bread cream
9 oz/250 g sourdough bread
2 shallots
Vegetable oil
⅔ cup/150 ml heavy cream
4 tsp unsalted butter
Salt, pepper

Bread chips
2 oz/60 g sourdough bread
2 tbsp vegetable oil
Salt

PREPARATION

Bread cream

1. Preheat the oven to 425°F/220°C and line a baking sheet with parchment paper. Slice the bread into large cubes, spread them out on the sheet, and toast them in the oven until golden.

2. In the meantime, trim the shallots and cut into rings. Heat some oil in a saucepan and sauté the shallots until golden brown. Stir in the toasted bread cubes, cream, and 1½ cups/350 ml water, then bring to a boil.

3. Combine the bread mixture with the butter in the blender jar and puree until creamy. Season with salt and pepper to taste, then cover and set aside until ready to serve.

Bread chips

1. Using a bread knife, cut the bread into paper-thin slices. Heat the oil in a skillet and fry the slices until crispy. Drain on paper towels and lightly salt.

Lentil salad
⅓ cup/80 g beluga lentils
Salt
1 red potato
2 small celery stalks
1 carrot
1 shallot
1 tbsp vegetable oil
Grated zest from ½ organic lemon
1 tsp balsamic vinegar
Pepper, sugar
3 sprigs parsley

Other
Blender (such as a Vitamix Pro 750)
Pastry bag with nozzle

Lentil salad

1. Simmer the lentils in salted water over medium heat for 15 minutes until just tender, then pour into a sieve to drain.

2. Trim and/or peel the potato, celery, carrot, and shallots, then cut into ¼-inch/5-mm dice. Heat the oil in a skillet and lightly sauté the vegetables. Add the lentils, toss lightly to mix, and remove from the heat.

3. Add the lemon zest and vinegar, then season the salad with salt, pepper, and sugar to taste. Wash the parsley and shake dry, then finely chop and stir into the salad.

TO SERVE

Divide the lentil salad into two bowls. Scoop the bread cream into the pastry bag and squeeze out dabs of the cream onto the salad (alternatively, you can use two spoons to add dollops of the cream to the salad). Arrange the bread chips alongside the salad.

PEAR, BEAN & BACON

SERVES 2

INGREDIENTS

Pear and green bean puree
9 oz/250 g green beans
⅞ cup/200 ml pear juice
Salt
3 sprigs summer savory
1 tbsp instant flour
½ tsp matcha powder
Salt, pepper, sugar

Bean & bacon
4 oz/125 g edamame in the pod
Salt
3½ oz/100 g smoked bacon
1 pear

Other
Blender (such as a Vitamix Pro 750)

PREPARATION

Pear and green bean puree
1. Wash and trim the green beans. In a saucepan, bring the pear juice and ½ cup/100 ml water to a boil. Blanch the green beans in the mixture for 5 minutes, then plunge the beans into ice water before refrigerating.

2. Stir the instant flour into the bean broth and let thicken slightly, then let cool somewhat.

3. Wash the savory, shake dry, then remove the leaves. Combine the bean broth and beans in the blender jar and puree until creamy. Blend in the savory leaves and matcha powder, then add salt, pepper, and sugar to taste.

Bean & bacon
1. Cook the edamame in boiling salted water for 5 minutes. Afterwards, drain in a colander and shell the edamame beans.

2. Cut the bacon into thin slices. Wash the pear, slice in half, and remove the core. Cut the halves lengthwise into very thin slices.

TO SERVE

Fan out the slices of each pear half, form into a ring, and place in the two bowls. Scoop the puree into the ring of pear slices and arrange the edamame beans on top. Garnish with the bacon.

Bowl: studio1.berlin

HEAVEN & EARTH

SERVES 3

INGREDIENTS

Parsley mayonnaise
8 sprigs parsley
1 large egg yolk
4 tsp milk
6 tbsp canola oil
Grated zest from ½ organic lemon
Salt, pepper, sugar

Pickled onion
1 red onion
3 tbsp apple cider vinegar
5 allspice berries
2 bay leaves
Salt, sugar

Onion rings
2 shallots
2 tbsp all-purpose flour
6 tbsp vegetable oil

Caramel apple
1 red apple
2 tbsp sugar
1 tbsp unsalted butter
3 tbsp apple juice

PREPARATION

Parsley mayonnaise
1. Wash the parsley, spin dry, and pick off the leaves. In a tall container, puree the leaves, egg yolk, and milk with an immersion blender. With the blender running, slowly add the oil until the mixture comes together. Add the lemon zest, season the mayonnaise with salt, pepper, and sugar to taste, and refrigerate until ready to serve.

Pickled onion
1. Peel the onion and cut into wedges. Combine the vinegar with 3 tablespoons water, allspice, bay leaves, and salt and sugar to taste in a saucepan and bring to a boil. Add the onion wedges, remove the pan from the heat, and set aside until ready to serve.

Onion rings
1. Peel the shallots, slice into rings, and dredge in the flour. Heat the oil in a skillet and fry the onion rings until golden brown. Drain on paper towels.

Caramel apple
1. Wash and core the apple. Cut the apple crosswise into rings ¼ inch/6 mm thick.

2. Melt the sugar in a frying pan. Add the butter and then the apple rings and cook until caramelized. Deglaze the pan with the apple juice and simmer for 2 minutes. Set aside until ready to serve.

Potato roesti and Cajun sausage
1 lb/450 g potatoes
1 large egg
2 ½ tbsp flour
Salt, pepper
Grated nutmeg
2 sprigs parsley
Vegetable oil
4 oz/120 g boudin noir
  (Cajun blood sausage)

For serving
Sprouts or microgreens

Other
Immersion blender

Potato roesti and Cajun sausage

1. Wash the potatoes (do not peel), and then grate them. Mix together the potatoes, egg, and flour and season with salt, pepper, and nutmeg to taste. Wash the parsley and spin dry. Chop the leaves and combine with the potato mixture.

2. Heat a little oil in a skillet. Squeeze the potato mixture, form six balls with a spoon, and arrange them in the pan. Gently flatten each ball and fry on both sides until golden brown. Remove from the pan.

3. Slice the sausage ¼ inch/5 mm thick and lightly fry on both sides in a little oil.

TO SERVE

Place some of the parsley mayonnaise in three bowls and add the roesti patties, one in each bowl. Layer the sausage slices and apple rings on top and cover with a second roesti patty. Add the onion rings and pickled onions, and sprinkle cress on top.

SALT-CRUSTED BEETS

SERVES 2

INGREDIENTS

3 medium egg whites
2 lb/1 kg coarse sea salt
1 lb/500 g beets

For serving
4 tbsp olive oil
Salt, pepper
Freshly grated horseradish

PREPARATION

1. Preheat the oven to 350°F/180°C. Whip the egg whites until stiff, then mix with the salt and scrape into a large casserole. You can alternatively pile the salt mixture on a baking sheet lined with parchment paper.

2. Wash and trim the beets, then place them in the salt and cover them completely with the salt mixture. Bake the beets for about 1 hour 40 minutes.

TO SERVE

Crack open the salt crust and remove the beets. Cut up the beets and divide them into two bowls. Drizzle with the olive oil, season with salt and pepper to taste, and sprinkle with grated horseradish.

ŒUFS COCOTTE

SERVES 2

INGREDIENTS

1 apple
½ onion
2 tbsp sugar
4 tsp apple cider vinegar
1 tbsp unsalted butter
Grated zest from ⅓ organic lemon
3½ oz/100 g Comté
  (French alpine cheese)
3 tbsp crème fraîche
1 tbsp quince mustard
  (or Dijon mustard)
6 medium eggs
Salt, pepper

For serving
1 scallion

Other
2 small ovensafe skillets or gratin dishes

PREPARATION

1. Preheat the oven to 300°F/150°C. Wash, peel, and core the apple, then cut in half. Peel the onion and cut the onion and the apple into wedges.

2. Melt the sugar in a saucepan and cook until golden brown. Add the apple and onion wedges along with the vinegar, butter, and lemon zest. Simmer the apple and onion wedges over low heat for 5 minutes.

3. Divide the apple and onion wedges into the small skillets. Cut the Comté into slices about ⅛ inch/4 mm thick and layer on top.

4. Add the crème fraîche and mustard to the pans, then crack three eggs into each pan. Season with salt and pepper to taste. Bring some water to a boil and pour about ⅓ inch/1 cm of water into a baking pan for a water bath. Set the small pans in the water bath and carefully slide into the oven. Cook the eggs until they are set, 10 to 15 minutes.

TO SERVE

Trim and wash the scallion, then thinly slice lengthwise and sprinkle on top of the eggs before serving.

BEEF TATAKI, SHIMEJI MUSHROOMS & HERB EMULSION

SERVES 2

INGREDIENTS

Tataki
6 oz/180 g beef tenderloin
1 tbsp soy sauce
1 tsp sake (Japanese rice wine)
1 tsp lime juice
Canola oil
Salt, pepper
Grated zest of ½ organic lime
1 cup radish sprouts

Shimeji mushrooms
¼ cup/70 ml sake (Japanese rice wine)
2 tbsp Japanese rice vinegar
Salt, sugar
2 oz/50 g shimeji mushrooms
  (or oyster mushrooms)

PREPARATION

Tataki
1. Let the beef stand at room temperature for about 10 minutes.

2. Whisk together the soy sauce, sake, and lime juice. Add the tenderloin and marinate for 10 minutes, turning several times.

3. Heat some oil in a skillet. Remove the tenderloin from the marinade and brown on all sides. Remove from the pan and let rest for 5 minutes.

4. Season the tenderloin all over with salt, pepper, and lime zest and cut into slices approximately ⅛ inch/3 mm thick. Place some radish sprouts on each slice and roll up.

Shimeji mushrooms
1. Combine the sake, vinegar, and salt and sugar to taste in a saucepan and bring to a boil. Add the mushrooms, cover the pot, and simmer until ready to serve.

Herb emulsion
1 sprig dill
1 sprig basil
1 sprig mint
4 sprigs chervil
5 sprigs fresh cilantro
¼ cup/60 ml milk
Grated zest of ½ organic lemon
Salt, pepper, sugar
2 tbsp heavy cream
¾ cup/170 ml canola oil

For serving
4 blackberries
Sesame seeds

Other
Blender (such as a Vitamix Pro 750)

Herb emulsion

1. Wash the herbs, spin dry, and remove the leaves.

2. Combine the leaves with the milk and lemon zest in the blender jar. Add salt, pepper, and sugar to taste and puree.

3. Add the cream and, with the motor running, slowly add the oil until the herb mixture emulsifies (comes together). Then pass the emulsion through a sieve.

TO SERVE

Arrange the tataki rolls with the mushrooms in two bowls. Wash the blackberries, pat dry, cut in half and add to the bowls. Sprinkle with sesame seeds and add the herb emulsion.

WINTER ROLL

SERVES 2

INGREDIENTS

Cabbage rounds
¼ red cabbage
Walnut oil
Salt, pepper

Rolls
1 oz/40 g red cabbage
1 oz/30 g apple (Elstar or
 Golden Delicious)
1 tbsp apple cider vinegar
Salt, pepper, sugar
Ground cinnamon
1 boneless duck breast
2 rice paper wrappers (available at
 Asian markets)

Red currant vinaigrette
1 oz/ 30 g red currants
1 tbsp apple cider vinegar
2 tbsp walnut oil
1 tsp honey
Salt, pepper

TO SERVE

Arrange the cabbage rounds in
two bowls, place the rolls on top
and drizzle the red currant
vinaigrette over each portion.

PREPARATION

Cabbage rounds
1. Preheat the oven to 400°F/200°C. Line a baking sheet
   with parchment paper. Wash the cabbage and cut
   the quarter head into two slices, ½ inch/1.5 cm thick.
   Drizzle with walnut oil, place on the baking sheet and roast
   for 10 to 15 minutes, until cooked through. Remove from
   the oven and season with salt and pepper.

Rolls
1. Wash the cabbage and apple and cut into strips.
   Marinate the strips in a mixture of vinegar, salt, pepper,
   sugar, and cinnamon to taste.

2. Decrease the oven temperature to 375°F/190°C.
   Heat a skillet and sear the duck breast with the skin side
   down. Place the pan in the oven and cook the duck
   for 5 minutes, or until done. Remove from the oven and
   let rest for another 5 minutes, then cut the duck breast
   lengthwise into strips.

3. Soak the rice paper in cold water until soft.
   Arrange the duck strips and cabbage/apple strips on
   the rice paper and roll up.

Red currant vinaigrette
1. Wash the currants, pat dry and strip the berries from
   the stems. Whisk together the vinegar, oil, and honey and
   season with salt and pepper to taste. Stir in the berries.

ASIAN CARBONARA

SERVES 3

INGREDIENTS

Meat
6½ tbsp sugar
⅓ cup/70 ml soy sauce
¼ cup/50 ml sake (Japanese rice wine)
2 tsp Japanese rice vinegar
2 stalks lemongrass
1 tsp fresh ginger
1 garlic clove
½ chile pepper
6 sprigs cilantro
2 star anise pods
1 cinnamon stick
Grated zest of ½ organic lemon
9 oz/250 g pork belly
Vegetable oil

Radish
1 black radish
2 tsp Japanese rice vinegar
Salt, sugar

Noodles
6 oz/180 g soba noodles
2 medium egg yolks

For serving
1 scallion
½ chile pepper

PREPARATION

Meat
1. Melt the sugar in a saucepan and cook until golden brown. Add the soy sauce, sake, rice vinegar, and 1¾ cups/400 ml water and bring to a boil.

2. Trim the lemongrass, peel the ginger and the garlic, and wash the chile pepper and the cilantro. Add it all to the broth together with the star anise, cinnamon stick, and lemon zest. Place the pork belly in the broth and simmer, covered, over low heat for about 1½ hours.

3. Remove the meat and cut into small pieces. Measure out ⅞ cup/200 ml of the broth, pour it through a sieve and set aside.

4. Heat some vegetable oil in a skillet and fry the pieces of pork belly until crispy.

Radish
1. Wash the radish and cut into thin slices. Marinate the radish slices in rice vinegar, salt, and sugar to taste.

Noodles
1. Bring a large pot of water to a boil, and cook the soba noodles until al dente. Drain the noodles.

2. Stir the egg yolks into the broth you set aside earlier, then add the noodles.

TO SERVE
Trim and wash the scallion, then slice diagonally into very thin rings. Wash the chile pepper and cut lengthwise into thin strips. Divide the noodles and meat into three bowls. Garnish with marinated radish, scallion, and chile.

ROASTED POTATO SOUP & PICKLED LEEKS

SERVES 2

INGREDIENTS

Soup
1 medium potato
2 small carrots
1 shallot
½ celery stalk
Vegetable oil
½ cup/100 ml heavy cream
   (or soy creamer for a vegan alternative)
Salt, pepper

Pickled leek
2 oz/60 g leek
Vegetable oil
Apple cider vinegar
Salt, pepper

For serving
Walnut oil

Other
Blender (such as a Vitamix Pro 750)

PREPARATION

Soup
1. Wash, peel, and cut the potato into large dice. Peel and dice the carrots and shallot. Wash, trim, and dice the celery.

2. Heat some oil in a saucepan and brown the potato on all sides. Add the carrots and celery and continue to sauté for 1 minute.

3. Add the shallot and pour in 1¾ cups/400 ml water. Bring the soup to a boil, then reduce the heat and simmer until the vegetables are tender.

4. Pour the cream in the blender jar and puree the soup. Season with salt and pepper to taste.

Pickled leek
Trim the roots and dark green tops from the leek, wash it, then cut diagonally into ⅓-inch/1-cm slices. Heat some oil in a skillet and sauté the leek slices. Pour in a bit of apple cider vinegar to finish and season the leek with salt and pepper to taste.

TO SERVE

Ladle the soup into two bowls, drizzle with a bit of walnut oil, and garnish with the pickled leek.

Bowl: Royal Copenhagen

VEGETABLE CURRY & COUSCOUS

SERVES 2

INGREDIENTS

Curry
½ inch/12 mm fresh ginger
1 garlic clove
½ tsp coriander seeds
3 cardamom pods
5 cloves
1 stalk lemongrass
1 oz/20 g leek
2 oz/50 g zucchini
2½ oz/70 g eggplant
2 oz/50 g green bell pepper
2 oz/50 g broccoli
2 oz/50 g snow peas
2 oz/50 g okra
Vegetable oil
1 tsp green curry paste
⅔ cup/150 ml coconut milk
2 kaffir lime leaves
Salt, sugar, fish sauce

Couscous
⅔ cup/120 g couscous
5 sprigs cilantro
2 tbsp sesame oil
Salt, pepper

PREPARATION

Curry
1. Peel the ginger and the garlic. Using a mortar and pestle, mash together the coriander seeds, cardamom, cloves, ginger, and garlic. Trim and chop the lemongrass and add to the spice mixture.

2. Wash, trim, and chop the vegetables. Heat some oil in a saucepan and sauté the spice mixture. Add the coconut milk, curry paste, and ⅔ cup/150 ml water.

3. Add the kaffir lime leaves and simmer the vegetables over low heat until tender. Season the curry with salt, sugar, and fish sauce to taste, then set aside for 30 minutes.

Couscous
1. In a small saucepan, bring ⅓ cup/70 ml water to a boil. Stir in the couscous, turn off the heat, and let sit for 10 minutes.

2. Wash and shake dry the cilantro, then chop. Stir the cilantro and sesame oil into the couscous, then season with salt and pepper to taste.

TO SERVE

Reheat the curry. Divide the couscous into two bowls, creating a hollow in the middle, then ladle the curry into the couscous.

Bowl: studio1.berlin

CODFISH PHÔ

SERVES 2

INGREDIENTS

Phô
8 oz/250 g skin-on cod fillet
5 oz/170 g soup vegetables (mixture of
   carrot, leek, celeriac, parsley)
4 springs fresh cilantro
2 star anise pods
1 cinnamon stick
Grated zest from ½ organic lime
Salt, sugar, fish sauce
Juice of ½ lime
8 oz/200 g rice noodles

Vegetables
4 sprigs fresh cilantro
1 oz/30 g mung bean sprouts
1 ½ oz/40 g carrots

For serving
Freshly grated horseradish

TO SERVE

Divide the noodles between two bowls.
Arrange the cod and vegetables on top
and pour the broth over them.
Place some horseradish on the fish.

PREPARATION

Phô
1. Rinse the cod in cold water, pat dry, and remove and
   reserve the skin. Divide the fish into two fillets
   (3 ounces/90 g each) and keep the fish trimmings.
   Wash and trim the soup vegetables and chop into
   rough dice. Wash the cilantro and spin dry.

2. Place the fish skin and trimmings, soup vegetables, cilantro,
   star anise, cinnamon, lime zest, 3 cups/800 ml of water,
   and salt, sugar, and fish sauce to taste in a large saucepan.
   Bring to a boil and simmer over very low heat for 1 hour.

3. Remove the pan from the stove and allow to steep for
   another 30 minutes. Clarify the broth by passing it
   through a sieve lined with cheesecloth or paper towels.

4. Season the broth with lime juice and salt, sugar, and
   fish sauce to taste and reheat to around 140°F/60°C.
   Add the fish, remove the pan from the heat, and allow it
   to steep for 7 to 10 minutes until cooked through.

5. Meanwhile, place the rice noodles in a pot of boiling
   salted water and cook until al dente.

Vegetables
1. Wash the cilantro, spin dry, and remove the leaves.
   Rinse the sprouts in cold water and drain. Peel the carrots
   and cut into a fine julienne. Mix everything together.

ASPARAGUS CAPPUCCINO

SERVES 4

INGREDIENTS

Vegetable coffee jus
10 oz/300 g soup vegetables
   (mixture of carrot, leek,
   celeriac, parsley)
Vegetable oil
1 tsp tomato paste
½ cup/100 ml apple juice
5 allspice berries
2 bay leaves
2–4 tbsp instant flour
1 tsp instant coffee powder
Salt, pepper, sugar

Mashed potatoes
1 lb/500 g red potatoes
Salt
4 tsp butter
Pepper, sugar

PREPARATION

Vegetable coffee jus
1. Wash, trim, and coarsely dice the soup vegetables.
   Heat some oil in a saucepan and brown the chopped
   vegetables. Add the tomato paste and briefly sauté
   before adding the apple juice, 2 cups/500 ml water,
   allspice, and bay leaves, then simmer over low heat
   for 1 hour.

2. Strain the stock through a sieve, then return it to
   a boil. Stir in the instant flour and thicken the stock.
   Season with the coffee powder and salt, pepper,
   and sugar to taste.

Mashed potatoes
1. Wash the potatoes and boil them, unpeeled, in salted
   water until tender. Drain and coarsely mash using
   a potato masher. Season with salt, pepper, and sugar
   to taste.

Hollandaise sauce

6 tbsp unsalted butter

2 large egg yolks

3 tbsp apple juice

2 tsp apple cider vinegar

Salt, pepper, sugar

Red pepper flakes

Asparagus

8 spears white asparagus

4 tsp unsalted butter

For serving

Sprouts (such as alfalfa sprouts
  and chickweed)

Hollandaise sauce

1. Melt the butter and set aside. For the water bath,
   bring some water to a boil in a large saucepan.
   In a stainless-steel bowl, whisk together the egg yolks,
   apple juice, and vinegar.

2. Place the bowl over the hot water bath and whisk
   the mixture until creamy. Remove the bowl from
   the water bath and slowly stir in the melted butter
   until the sauce thickens. (If you add the butter
   too quickly, the sauce may separate.) Season to taste
   with salt, pepper, sugar, and red pepper flakes.

Asparagus

1. Peel the asparagus and cut 1 inch/3 cm off the ends
   before thinly slicing the spears. Heat the butter in
   a skillet and brown the asparagus. Pour in the vegetable
   coffee jus.

TO SERVE

Spoon the mashed potatoes into four bowls or glasses
and ladle in the asparagus ragout. Top with the hollandaise
sauce and garnish with sprouts.

STEAMED DUMPLINGS

SERVES 3

INGREDIENTS

Dough
1⅔ cups/200 g all-purpose flour
½ tsp baking powder
¼ cup/50 g sugar
2 tbsp/30 ml vegetable oil
Salt

Filling
½ cup/50 g textured vegetable protein
  (TVP)
1 large carrot
¼ tsp sugar
2 tsp sake (Japanese rice wine)
2 tsp soy sauce
2 tsp teriyaki sauce
1 tsp Japanese rice vinegar
½ tsp all-purpose flour
Salt
Lime juice
5 sprigs cilantro

For serving
3 tbsp/30 g salted peanuts
2 scallions

Other
Steamer basket or steamer insert

PREPARATION

Dough
1. Combine the flour, baking powder, sugar, oil, ⅓ cup/80 ml water, and salt to taste, then knead into a smooth dough. Cover the dough and let rest for 10 minutes.

Filling
1. Prepare the textured vegetable protein according to the package instructions. Peel the carrot and cut into ¼-inch/5-mm dice.

2. Melt the sugar in a saucepan and cook until golden brown. Add the diced carrot followed by the sake, soy sauce, teriyaki sauce, and rice vinegar. Sprinkle in the flour while stirring constantly, then season with salt and lime juice to taste. Remove from the heat and stir in the drained textured vegetable protein.

3. Wash the cilantro and shake dry, then chop the leaves. Stir into the filling.

4. Divide the dough into pieces weighing 1½ oz/40 g each. Press the pieces flat, top each with 1 tbsp of the filling, then fold the dough closed and form them into dumplings.

5. Place the dumplings in the steamer basket. Heat some water in a pot, set the steamer basket on top, and steam the dumplings for 10 minutes.

TO SERVE

Chop the peanuts. Wash the scallions and slice into thin rings. Arrange the dumplings in three bowls and sprinkle with the peanuts and scallions.

RADICCHIO SALAD, CHORIZO, RICOTTA & DATES

SERVES 2

INGREDIENTS

Radicchio
2 heads radicchio (ideally
  Treviso Tardivo)
¼ cup/60 ml olive oil
1 tsp honey
Grated zest from ½ organic orange
Salt, pepper
¼ cup/20 g pecans
Sugar
2 tsp white balsamic vinegar

Chorizo
3 oz/90 g chorizo
Olive oil

For serving
2 dates
3 oz/80 g ricotta salata
  (or mild feta cheese)

PREPARATION

Radicchio
1. Wash the radicchio and separate the heads into individual leaves. Marinate half the leaves with 2 tbsp of the olive oil, the honey, orange zest, and salt and pepper to taste.

2. Heat the remaining oil in a skillet and briefly sauté the remaining leaves along with the pecans. Season with salt, pepper, and sugar to taste and then add the vinegar.

Chorizo
1. Cut the chorizo into ⅛-inch/4-mm-thick slices. Thinly coat a second skillet with oil and brown the slices well on each side.

TO SERVE

Remove the pits from the dates and cut them lengthwise into thin strips. Alternately layer the marinated radicchio and the sautéed radicchio in two bowls. Coarsely crumble the ricotta over the radicchio, then add the dates and the warm chorizo.

Bowl: studio1.berlin

CHARD EGG
& CREAMED POTATOES

SERVES 2

INGREDIENTS

Chard egg
6 chard leaves
Salt, pepper
Vegetable oil
2 medium eggs

PREPARATION

Chard egg
1. Wash the chard and remove the thick stem from the leaves. Blanch the leaves in boiling salted water for 30 seconds, then plunge the chard into a bowl of ice water.

2. On paper towels, spread three chard leaves out flat to form a circle (about 6 inches/15 cm wide). Spread another paper towel over the top and use a rolling pin to roll the circle of chard out flat. Repeat with more paper towels and the remaining three chard leaves.

3. Roll out about 20 inches/50 cm of plastic wrap and brush lightly with oil. Cut the plastic wrap in half and position a circle of chard on each half, then carefully remove the paper towel.

4. Gently slide one piece of the plastic wrap with a circle of chard into a small bowl and then crack an egg into the chard circle. Season with salt and pepper to taste. Repeat with the second chard circle and egg.

5. Gently fold the chard leaves over the egg, carefully gathering the plastic wrap and twisting the ends together and using some kitchen twine to tie the plastic wrap closed. Repeat this process with the second egg. Cook the chard eggs in simmering water for 5 to 7 minutes.

Creamed potatoes
4 large potatoes
1 shallot
1 scallion
1 tsp butter
4 tsp white wine
1 cup/250 ml heavy cream
5 tsp grated Parmesan
Grated zest from ⅓ organic lemon
Salt, pepper, sugar
Grated nutmeg

For serving
2 bacon slices
Freshly chopped parsley

Other
Kitchen twine

Creamed potatoes

1. Peel the potatoes and cut them into ¼-inch/6-mm dice. Peel the shallot and finely dice. Wash and trim the scallion before slicing into thin rings.

2. Melt the butter in a saucepan and sauté the shallot. Add the diced potatoes and the wine. Gradually pour in the cream and cook the potatoes until just tender.

3. Remove the potatoes from the heat, stir in the Parmesan and scallion, then season with the lemon zest and salt, pepper, sugar, and nutmeg to taste.

TO SERVE

Cut the bacon into strips and fry in a skillet until crispy. Spoon the creamed potatoes into two bowls. Slice open and remove the plastic wrap, then season the chard eggs again with salt. Place a chard egg on the potatoes in each bowl, then top with the bacon and garnish with parsley.

UDON NOODLES & SOY CARAMEL

INGREDIENTS

Soy caramel
1½ tbsp sugar
2½ tbsp sake (Japanese rice wine)
2 tbsp soy sauce
1 tbsp fish sauce
1 tbsp teriyaki sauce
2 tbsp sesame seeds

Udon noodles
Salt
14 oz/400 g udon noodles
2 oz/60 g carrots
2 oz/60 g snow peas
1 tbsp sesame oil
2 tbsp butter
1 tbsp lime juice
Grated zest from ½ organic lime

For serving
1 scallion
1 tbsp sesame seeds

PREPARATION

Soy caramel
1. Melt the sugar in a saucepan and cook until golden brown. Stir in the sake, soy sauce, fish sauce, and teriyaki sauce and simmer for 5 minutes. Stir in the sesame seeds and set the caramel aside.

Udon noodles
1. Bring a large pot of salted water to a boil, add the noodles, and cook until al dente. Pour the noodles into a colander and let drain.

2. Peel the carrots, then wash and trim the snow peas. Thinly slice the carrots and the snow peas.

3. Heat the sesame oil in a skillet and brown the vegetables. Add the soy caramel, noodles, butter, lime juice, and lime zest and toss lightly to mix.

TO SERVE

Wash and trim the scallion, then slice into thin rings. Divide the noodles into two bowls and garnish with the scallion and sesame seeds.

Bowl: studio1.berlin

POACHED SALMON
& SORREL STOCK

SERVES 2

INGREDIENTS

Stock
1½ oz/50 g sorrel
2½ oz/70 g avocado
Scant ½ cup/100 ml apple juice
Salt, pepper, sugar

Salmon
9 oz/250 g soup vegetables (mixture of
   carrot, leek, celeriac, parsley)
5 allspice berries
2 bay leaves
½ tsp coriander seeds
Salt
7 oz/200 g skin-on salmon fillet
Vegetable oil

Salad
5 radishes
4 oz/120 g cucumber
Grated zest from ¼ organic lemon
Salt

Other
Blender (such as a Vitamix Pro 750)

TO SERVE

Divide the salad into two bowls and
top with the poached salmon. Salt once
more, then place the fried salmon skin
on top and pour in the sorrel stock.

PREPARATION

Stock
1. Wash the sorrel and shake dry, then peel the avocado.
   Combine the sorrel and avocado with the apple juice
   and a scant ½ cup/100 ml water in the blender jar and
   puree until smooth. Season with salt, pepper, and sugar
   to taste, then refrigerate.

Salmon
1. Wash, trim and coarsely dice the soup vegetables.
   In a saucepan, combine the soup vegetables with
   3⅓ cups/800 ml water, the allspice, bay leaves, coriander,
   and salt to taste. Bring to a boil and simmer over low heat
   for 30 minutes, then let it sit for another 30 minutes.

2. While the broth is cooking, rinse the salmon in cold water,
   blot dry, and remove and set aside the skin. Divide the fish
   into two fillets. Fry the skin in some oil and lightly salt.

3. Pour the vegetable broth through a sieve into a second pot,
   then heat to about 140°F/60°C. Remove from the heat,
   place the salmon in the broth and let it sit for 5 to 8 minutes
   until fully cooked.

Salad
1. Clean, trim, and thinly slice the radishes. Peel the cucumber,
   cut in half lengthwise, remove the seeds, and cut into
   thin slices. Combine the sliced radishes and cucumber
   and season with the lemon zest and salt to taste.

Bowl: studio1.berlin

ASPARAGUS & PASSION FRUIT BASIL HOLLANDAISE SAUCE

SERVES 2

INGREDIENTS

Asparagus
16 spears white asparagus
½ organic lemon
4 tsp butter
Salt, sugar

Potato cubes
7 oz/200 g potatoes
Vegetable oil
Salt

Hollandaise sauce
4 oz/125 g butter
4 tsp orange juice
1 oz/30 g passion fruit pulp
  (from about 2 fruit)
2 medium egg yolks
3 sprigs basil
Salt, sugar, cayenne pepper

TO SERVE

Arrange the asparagus and the potato cubes in two bowls, then pour the hollandaise sauce over the asparagus.

PREPARATION

Asparagus
1. Peel the asparagus and cut 1 inch/3 cm off the ends. In a pot, bring an ample amount of water to a boil. Add the lemon and butter and season the water generously with salt and sugar.

2. Add the asparagus to the simmering water and slowly cook it until al dente.

Potato cubes
1. In the meantime, peel the potatoes and cut them into ⅜-inch/1-cm cubes. Add enough oil to cover the bottom of a skillet. Heat the oil, then fry the potato cubes until crispy. Spread the potato cubes on paper towels to drain and sprinkle with salt to taste.

Hollandaise sauce
1. Melt the butter and set aside. For the water bath, bring some water to a boil in a large saucepan. In a stainless-steel bowl, whisk together the orange juice, passion fruit pulp, and egg yolks.

2. Place the bowl over the hot water bath and whisk the egg yolk mixture until it is fluffy. Remove the bowl from the water bath and slowly stir in the melted butter until the sauce thickens. (If you add the butter too quickly, the sauce may separate.)

3. Wash the basil, shake it dry, and coarsely chop the leaves. Stir the basil into the hollandaise sauce and season to taste with salt, sugar, and cayenne pepper.

STUFFED CALAMARETTI & BEEFSTEAK TOMATO

SERVES 2

INGREDIENTS

Oven-dried tomato
1 beefsteak tomato
Salt, pepper

Calamaretti
2 oz/50 g black olives
2 sprigs thyme
6 calamaretti (baby calamari)
3 oz/90 g buffalo mozzarella
2 tbsp olive oil

For serving
3 tbsp olive oil
Grated zest from ½ organic lemon
Sprouts (clover, radish, or broccoli)

PREPARATION

Oven-dried tomato
1. Preheat the oven to 250°F/120°C. Line a baking sheet with parchment paper. Wash the tomato and slice crosswise ⅜ inch/1 cm thick. Place the tomato slices on the baking sheet and sprinkle with salt and pepper.

2. Allow the tomato slices to dry in the oven for about 1 hour. Every 10 minutes, open the oven door and allow the moisture to escape.

Calamaretti
1. Pit and finely chop the olives. Wash the thyme, spin dry and strip off the leaves. Combine with the olives. Clean the calamaretti and cut off the crown with the tentacles. Rinse the tentacles and mantle in cold water and pat dry.

2. Cut the mozzarella first into ⅜-inch/1-cm-thick slices and then into 1-inch/3-cm matchsticks. Place one mozzarella matchstick in each calamaretti mantle and stuff with the olives. Do not pack it too full, since the calamaretti will shrink during frying.

3. Heat the olive oil in a skillet over moderate heat and quickly fry the calamaretti on all sides. Add the tentacles last.

TO SERVE

Place one tomato slice in each of two bowls, drizzle with olive oil and sprinkle with lemon zest. Arrange the calamaretti on top and garnish with sprouts.

FRIED TOFU & PASSION FRUIT LEEK DIPPING SAUCE

SERVES 2

INGREDIENTS

Fried tofu
4 tsp fresh ginger
1 garlic clove
4 sprigs cilantro
6 tbsp all-purpose flour
Salt
10 oz/300 g tofu
Vegetable oil
1¾ cup/100 g panko bread crumbs

Dipping sauce
¾ cup/20 g spinach
½ oz/15 g leek greens
⅓ cup/75 ml passion fruit juice
1 tbsp all-purpose flour
Salt, pepper, sugar

Other
Blender (such as a Vitamix Pro 750)

PREPARATION

Fried tofu
1. Peel and mince the ginger and garlic. Wash the cilantro, shake dry, and chop the leaves.

2. In a bowl, combine 2½ tablespoons of the flour with ⅓ cup/80 ml water and mix until smooth, then season with salt to taste. Stir in the ginger, garlic, and cilantro.

3. Cut the tofu into slices, salt, and then coat in the remaining flour.

4. In a pot, heat an ample amount of oil to 325°F/170°C. Pour the panko into a second bowl. First dip the tofu slices in the ginger mixture, then coat them in the panko. In batches, fry them in the hot oil until golden, then drain on paper towels.

Dipping sauce
1. Wash the spinach and leek greens and shake dry. Combine the passion fruit juice and flour in a saucepan and bring to a boil, stirring constantly. Transfer the juice to the blender jar, add the spinach and leek greens, and puree until creamy. Season with salt, pepper, and sugar to taste.

TO SERVE

Arrange the fried tofu slices in two bowls and serve hot with the dipping sauce.

SEA BASS, CELERY
& CHILI STRAWBERRIES

SERVES 2

INGREDIENTS

Celery sticks
2 celery stalks
4 tsp butter
3 tbsp apple juice
Salt, pepper, sugar

Sea bass
2 skin-on sea bass fillets
  (3 oz/90 g each)
1 sprig tarragon
Olive oil
4 tsp butter
2 tsp vermouth

Chili strawberries
4 strawberries
Red pepper flakes
½ tsp olive oil
2 tsp butter

For serving
Tarragon leaves
Sea salt

PREPARATION

Celery sticks
1. Peel the celery and cut the stalks into pieces about
   3 inches/8 cm long and then into matchsticks.

2. Heat the butter in a saucepan and sauté the celery sticks.
   Deglaze the pan with apple juice, cook over medium heat
   for 1 minute, and set aside.

Sea bass
1. Meanwhile, rinse the fish fillets in cold water, pat dry,
   and remove any remaining bones. Wash the tarragon
   and spin dry.

2. Heat some olive oil in a skillet and fry the fish fillets,
   skin side down, until crispy. Add the butter, tarragon,
   and vermouth, and toss the fish in the sauce.

Chili strawberries
1. While the fish is frying, wash and trim the strawberries
   and cut in half. Sprinkle the strawberry halves with
   pepper flakes and fry, cut side down, in oil in a second
   skillet. Add the butter and set the berries aside.

TO SERVE

Divide the celery sticks and broth between two bowls.
Arrange the fish on top and sprinkle with some sea salt.
Garnish with the strawberries and sprinkle with tarragon.

Bowl: studio1.berlin

COCONUT CHICKEN, BLACK SALSIFY & GOLDEN OYSTER MUSHROOMS

SERVES 2

INGREDIENTS

Chicken
1 stalk lemongrass
½ inch/12 mm fresh ginger
1⅓ cups/300 ml coconut milk
4 tsp sake (Japanese rice wine)
Salt
2 boneless, skinless chicken breasts

Pureed black salsify
7 oz/200 g black salsify
1 tbsp butter
½ cup/100 ml milk
Salt, pepper
Grated nutmeg

Salad
¾ cup/30 g chickweed
1 oz/30 g golden oyster mushrooms
2 tbsp olive oil
Juice of ½ organic lime
Salt, pepper

Other
Blender (such as a Vitamix Pro 750)

PREPARATION

Chicken
1. Trim the lemongrass, peel the ginger, and finely chop both vegetables. Combine with the coconut milk, sake, and salt to taste in a saucepan and bring to a boil. Add the chicken breasts, remove from the heat, and steep for 10 to 15 minutes, or until cooked through.

Pureed black salsify
1. Meanwhile, peel and wash the black salsify and chop into small pieces. Heat the butter in a saucepan and lightly sauté the chopped pieces.

2. Add the milk and cook the black salsify over low heat for 10 minutes until done. Transfer to the blender jar and puree until smooth, then season with salt, pepper, and nutmeg to taste.

Salad
1. Wash the chickweed and shake dry. Marinate the chickweed and mushrooms in the oil, lime juice, salt, and pepper to taste.

TO SERVE

Divide the pureed salsify between two bowls and place the chicken on top. Lightly salt and serve the salad on the side.

MANGO SPROUT SALAD

SERVES 4

INGREDIENTS

Salad
1 mango
1 carrot
7 oz/200 g mung bean sprouts
12 sprigs cilantro
1 scallion

Dressing
1 organic lime
2 tbsp fish sauce or soy sauce
2 tbsp sesame oil

For serving
Salted dry-roasted peanuts
¾ oz/20 g radish sprouts

PREPARATION

Salad
1. Peel the mango, cut the flesh away from the seed, and then thinly slice the mango. Peel and julienne the carrot.

2. Wash the sprouts and let them drain. Wash the cilantro, shake dry, and finely chop the leaves. Wash and trim the scallion, then slice it on the diagonal.

Dressing
1. Grate the zest from the lime and then juice the lime. Combine the lime zest and juice with the fish sauce and the sesame oil.

TO SERVE

Toss the mango, carrot, sprouts, cilantro, and scallion with the dressing. Let the salad sit for about 5 minutes, then divide it into four bowls. Garnish with peanuts and radish sprouts.

Bowl: ASA

CORN COBBLER

SERVES 2

INGREDIENTS

Corn coulis
7 oz/200 g canned or frozen corn
⅓ cup/80 ml heavy cream
2 tsp butter
Salt, red pepper flakes

Polenta
2 sprigs cilantro
⅞ cup/200 ml milk
½ tsp coriander seeds
3 tbsp coarse-ground instant polenta
1 tbsp grated Parmesan
Salt, pepper, sugar

Chicken
2 tbsp vegetable oil
9 oz/250 g corn-fed chicken breast
Salt

For serving
2 sprigs cilantro

Other
Blender (such as a Vitamix Pro 750)

PREPARATION

Corn coulis
1. In a saucepan, combine 6 oz/170 g corn with the cream and bring to a boil. Transfer to the blender jar, add the butter, and puree until smooth. Season the corn coulis with salt and pepper flakes to taste and set aside.

Polenta
1. Wash the cilantro and shake dry. In a saucepan, combine the milk, cilantro, and coriander seeds and bring to a boil; remove from the heat and let sit for about 20 minutes.

2. Strain the cilantro and milk mixture through a sieve and then bring the milk back to a boil. Whisk in the instant polenta and cook for 1 minute, stirring constantly, then let sit for 5 minutes. Stir in the Parmesan and season the polenta with salt, pepper, and sugar to taste.

Chicken
1. Heat the oil in a skillet and fry the chicken breast skin-side down until crispy, then turn it over and continue to fry until done. Salt the chicken breast.

TO SERVE

Reheat the corn coulis. Spoon the polenta into two bowls followed by the corn coulis. Cut the chicken into cubes and arrange on top. Wash the cilantro, shake dry, and sprinkle the leaves on top of the chicken as a garnish.

ASPARAGUS TEMPURA & SHISO MAYONNAISE

SERVES 2

INGREDIENTS

Mayonnaise
2 medium egg yolks
2 tsp sake (Japanese rice wine)
⅓ cup/70 g vegetable oil
1½ tbsp sesame oil
4 shiso leaves (available at
  Asian markets)
Salt

Tempura
10 spears green asparagus
½ cup/60 g tempura flour
  (available at Asian markets)
1 oz/20 g ice cubes
Salt
Vegetable oil

Other
Immersion blender

PREPARATION

Mayonnaise
1. Add the egg yolks and sake to a tall, narrow container. Using an immersion blender, slowly blend the mixture and drizzle in the oil and the sesame oil until the mayonnaise thickens.

2. Wash the shiso leaves and blot dry, then thinly slice. Stir into the mayonnaise and season with salt to taste.

Tempura
1. Cut 1 inch/3 cm off the bottom of the asparagus spears. Cut the spears in half, then roll the asparagus in some tempura flour.

2. Combine the remaining tempura flour with ⅓ cup/ 80 ml water and the ice cubes and mix into a smooth batter. Season with salt to taste.

3. Heat an ample amount of oil to 325°F/170°C in a pot. Dunk the asparagus pieces into the tempura batter and then fry in batches in the hot oil. Drain on paper towels.

TO SERVE

Arrange the asparagus in two bowls and serve with a side of the shiso mayonnaise for dipping.

POPPY SEED-CRUSTED SKREI & KOHLRABI

SERVES 2

INGREDIENTS

Poppy seed crust
3 tbsp softened butter
1 medium egg yolk
½ tsp mustard
2 sprigs tarragon
2½ tbsp bread crumbs
2 tbsp ground poppy seeds
Salt, pepper, sugar

Kohlrabi
½ cup/20 g wild garlic (also known as
  wild leek or ramps)
5 oz/140 g kohlrabi
2 tbsp butter
Salt, pepper, sugar
Grated nutmeg

Skrei
7 oz/200 g skrei (Norwegian or
  Atlantic cod) fillet
2 tbsp olive oil
1 tbsp butter
4 tsp vermouth

For serving
Grated zest of ½ organic lemon

TO SERVE

Reheat the kohlrabi and stir in the wild
garlic. Divide the vegetables between two
bowls and arrange the poppy seed–crusted
fish on top. Sprinkle with lemon zest.

PREPARATION

Poppy seed crust
1. Whisk the butter until creamy. Add the egg yolk and mustard. Wash the tarragon, spin dry, and roughly chop the leaves. Fold into the butter with the bread crumbs and poppy seeds. Season the poppy seed mixture with salt, pepper, and sugar to taste and spread onto parchment paper in a ¼-inch/ 6-mm-thick layer. Refrigerate.

Kohlrabi
1. Wash the wild garlic, spin dry, and set aside. Peel the kohlrabi and roughly chop.

2. Heat the butter in a saucepan and sauté the kohlrabi. Deglaze the pan with ¼ cup/60 ml of water and season with salt, pepper, sugar, and nutmeg to taste. Cook over medium heat for 2 minutes and set aside.

Skrei
1. Heat the oven to 350°F/180°C. Rinse the fish in cold water, pat dry, and remove the skin. Then divide the fish into two fillets.

2. Heat the oil in a skillet and fry the fillets on one side for about 2 minutes over medium heat. Transfer the skillet to the oven and continue cooking the fish for 4 minutes.

3. Meanwhile, cut the poppy seed crust into sections the size of the fillets. Return the skillet to the stovetop, place the crust on the fillets and add the butter and vermouth. Increase the oven temperature to 425°F/220°C, place the skillet in the oven and cook 1 to 2 minutes until the crust is browned.

Bowl: studio1.berlin

CRISPY CHICKEN LIVER, RHUBARB & MINT MASHED POTATOES

SERVES 2

INGREDIENTS

Stewed rhubarb
4 oz/125 g rhubarb
1 tbsp frozen raspberries
4 tsp sugar
2 tsp Grand Marnier
2 tsp Campari
¼ vanilla bean
1 strip each organic orange
  and lemon peel
Salt

Caramelized shallots
2 shallots
1 tbsp all-purpose flour
Canola oil
Salt

PREPARATION

Stewed rhubarb
1. Preheat the oven to 375°C/190°C. Wash the rhubarb, peel, and slice into pieces approximately 3 inches/7 cm long.

2. Combine the rhubarb, raspberries, sugar, Grand Marnier, Campari, vanilla bean, and orange and lemon peel in a casserole dish and season with salt to taste. Cover with aluminum foil and let the rhubarb stew in the oven for approximately 15 minutes.

3. Remove the pot from the oven and cool immediately in the fridge to stop the cooking process.

Caramelized shallots
1. Peel the shallots, slice into ⅛-inch/4-mm rings, and dredge in the flour.

2. Heat ½ inch/12 mm oil in a small saucepan and fry the rings until they turn golden brown. Drain on paper towels and season with salt.

Mint mashed potatoes
11 oz/320 g potatoes
Salt
1 tbsp butter
7 tbsp/100 ml milk
Pepper, grated nutmeg
2 sprigs mint

Chicken liver
8 oz/250 g chicken livers
Salt, pepper
1 tbsp all-purpose flour
Vegetable oil
5 tbsp puffed amaranth

Mint mashed potatoes

1. Peel the potatoes and boil in salted water until done. Drain and mash the potatoes with a masher.

2. Add the butter and milk to the potatoes and season with salt, pepper, and nutmeg to taste. Wash the mint, spin dry, and slice the leaves into fine strips. Fold into the mashed potatoes.

Chicken liver

1. Trim the livers, season with salt and pepper, and dredge in the flour.

2. Heat some oil in a frying pan and fry the livers, 1 minute on each side. Remove the pan from the heat and let the livers rest for another 2 minutes. Then dredge in the amaranth.

TO SERVE

Arrange three mounds of mint mashed potatoes and three pieces of rhubarb in two bowls. Place the livers and caramelized shallots on top and drizzle some of the rhubarb broth over the top.

VENUS CLAMS IN HARD CIDER

SERVES 2

INGREDIENTS

2 lb/1 kg Venus clams
5 oz/170 g soup vegetables (mixture of
  carrot, leek, celeriac, parsley)
½ green apple
Vegetable oil
¼ cup/100 ml hard cider
3 tbsp heavy cream
Grated zest of ½ organic lemon
Salt, pepper, sugar

PREPARATION

1. Rinse the clams thoroughly under cold running water.
   Discard any damaged clams and drain the rest in a sieve.

2. Wash and trim the soup vegetables. Peel, quarter, and
   core the apple. Cut the soup vegetables and apple into
   a fine julienne.

3. Heat some vegetable oil in a wide pot or Dutch oven.
   Add the clams, julienned vegetables and apples, cider,
   and cream. Season with lemon zest and salt, pepper,
   and sugar to taste.

4. Cover the pot and cook the clams for 3 to 5 minutes
   until they open. Discard any clams that fail to open.

TO SERVE

Arrange the clams with the vegetables and broth
in two bowls.

Bowl: Royal Copenhagen

WILD GARLIC TAGLIATELLE

SERVES 4

INGREDIENTS

Pasta dough
2½ cups/300 g all-purpose flour
3 medium eggs
2 tbsp olive oil
Salt

Wild garlic
2½ oz/70 g wild garlic (also known as wild leek or ramps)
1 oz/30 g slivered almonds
4 oz/120 g kohlrabi
Salt
Olive oil
3 tbsp butter
1 tbsp apple cider vinegar
Pepper, sugar

For serving
2 oz/60 g radishes

PREPARATION

Pasta dough
1. Combine the flour, eggs, oil, and salt to taste and knead into a smooth dough. Wrap the dough in plastic wrap and chill in the refrigerator for 30 minutes.

2. After the dough has chilled, roll it out into a large, paper-thin rectangle, then dust with flour. Starting from the long edge, roll the dough up. Cut the roll into strips ½ to ¾ inches/1 to 2 cm in width.

Wild garlic
1. Wash the wild garlic and shake dry. Toast the slivered almonds in a dry skillet. Peel the kohlrabi and cut into 1-inch/2.5-cm chunks.

2. Cook the pasta in a generous amount of boiling salted water for 3 to 4 minutes.

3. Heat some olive oil in a large skillet and brown the kohlrabi on all sides. Add the wild garlic and toss gently. Add the slivered almonds, butter, vinegar, and ⅓ cup/80 ml of the pasta water and bring it to a boil briefly.

4. Drain the pasta, then add it to the wild garlic in the pan. Gently toss everything together and season with salt, pepper, and sugar to taste.

TO SERVE

Wash and trim the radishes, then slice thinly. Divide the pasta into four bowls and garnish with the radishes.

CHILLED PEA SOUP
& NECTARINE YAKITORI SKEWERS

SERVES 2

INGREDIENTS

Soup
2 scallions
5 mint leaves
Coconut oil
1¾ cups/250 g frozen peas
3½ oz/100 ml coconut milk
7 oz/200 ml rice milk
Salt, pepper, sugar
Grated nutmeg
Grated zest from ½ organic lime

Yakitori skewers
1 nectarine
2 tbsp coconut oil
Grated zest from ½ organic lime
Salt, pepper, red pepper flakes

Other
Blender (such as a Vitamix Pro 750)
2 wooden skewers

TO SERVE

Divide the remaining peas into
two bowls. Pour the soup onto
the peas and arrange the nectarine
yakitori skewers on top.

PREPARATION

Soup
1. Wash, trim, and chop the scallions. Wash the mint and pat dry.

2. Heat some coconut oil in a saucepan and sauté the scallions. Add 1½ cups/200 g peas, then stir in the coconut milk and rice milk. Add the mint and season with salt, pepper, and sugar to taste.

3. Warm the mixture but do not boil, then let sit for 5 minutes. Use a blender to puree the mixture and then strain it through a fine sieve.

4. Season the soup with the lime zest and salt, pepper, and nutmeg to taste, then refrigerate until ready to serve.

5. Let the remaining peas thaw.

Yakitori skewers
1. Wash the nectarine, cut in half, and remove the pit. Cut the halves into triangular chunks and slide them onto the skewers.

2. Heat the coconut oil in a skillet and sauté the skewers on all sides until golden brown.

3. Remove the pan from the heat and season the skewers with the lime zest and salt, pepper, and pepper flakes to taste.

Bowl: studio1.berlin

PRAWNS FLAMBÉ & TOMATO CROSTINI

SERVES 2

INGREDIENTS

Tomato crostini
½ loaf ciabatta or other rustic bread
2 tomatoes
¼ orange
2 tbsp olive oil
Salt, pepper, sugar

Prawns
3 sprigs tarragon
1 garlic clove
10 prawns or jumbo shrimp
Olive oil
3 tbsp cognac
2 tbsp butter
2 tsp tomato paste
⅓ cup/80 ml heavy cream
Salt, sugar

PREPARATION

Tomato crostini

1. Slice the ciabatta ⅜ inch/1 cm thick and toast the slices. Wash the tomatoes, cut into quarters, and remove the seeds. Dice the tomato quarters. Segment the orange by cutting the flesh away from the membranes and dice.

2. Combine the tomatoes, orange, and oil and season with salt, pepper, and sugar to taste.

Prawns

1. Wash the tarragon and spin dry. Peel and slice the garlic. Rinse the prawns under cold water and pat dry.

2. Heat a little oil in a skillet and lightly sauté the prawns on both sides. Drizzle with the cognac and toss the prawns briefly; remove from the heat and carefully ignite the alcohol with a long lit match.

3. Return to the heat, add the butter, tomato paste, tarragon, and garlic, and toss to combine. Deglaze the pan with the cream and season with salt and sugar to taste.

TO SERVE

Divide the tomato mixture between the toasted ciabatta slices. Arrange the prawns in two bowls or pour directly from the pan. Serve the tomato crostini on the side.

CELERIAC PEAR FLAN
& OVEN-ROASTED ONIONS

SERVES 2

INGREDIENTS

Oven-roasted onions
6 cipollini onions
2 tbsp apple cider vinegar
2 bay leaves
5 allspice berries
Salt, sugar

Flan
6 oz/170 g celeriac
3 oz/90 g pear
1 shallot
4 tsp butter
4 tsp vermouth
8 tsp white wine
⅞ cup/200 ml heavy cream
Salt, pepper, sugar
Grated nutmeg
3 medium eggs

Celeriac chips
2 oz/60 g celeriac
½ cup/100 ml vegetable oil
Salt

Other
Blender (such as a Vitamix Pro 750)

TO SERVE

Remove the onions from the stock and slice in half. Arrange on top of the flan along with the celeriac chips.

PREPARATION

Oven-roasted onions

1. Preheat the oven to 425°F/220°C, then line a baking sheet with parchment paper. Peel the onions, place them on the baking sheet, and roast them for 15 to 20 minutes, or until they start to take on color.

2. In a saucepan, combine ¼ cup/60 ml water with the vinegar, bay leaves, allspice, and salt and sugar to taste and bring to a boil. Place the onions in the stock and set aside.

Flan

1. Peel and coarsely chop the celeriac, pear, and shallot. Heat the butter in a saucepan and sauté the chopped vegetables and pear. Add the vermouth and white wine to deglaze, then pour in the cream and ⅞ cup/200 ml water. Bring to a boil, then simmer over low heat until tender.

2. Add the celeriac mixture to the blender jar and puree until creamy. Season with salt, pepper, sugar, and nutmeg to taste. Mix in the eggs.

3. Reduce the heat of the oven to 250°F/125°C. Slide a deep baking pan into the oven and fill with 1 inch/2.5 cm hot water. Pour the cream into two bowls, set in the water bath, and bake for 40 to 50 minutes.

Celeriac chips

1. Peel the celeriac and thinly slice (1 mm thick). Heat the oil in a small saucepan and fry the slices until golden. Drain on paper towels and lightly salt.

MISO ASPARAGUS, TOMATO BEURRE BLANC & CILANTRO

SERVES 2

INGREDIENTS

Asparagus
⅓ cup/60 g sugar
6 tbsp miso
4 tsp sake (Japanese rice wine)
4 tsp fish sauce
4 tsp soy sauce
10 spears green asparagus

Beurre blanc
7 oz/200 g tomatoes
3½ oz/100 g unsalted butter, cold
2 tbsp sake (Japanese rice wine)
1 tbsp Japanese rice vinegar
Salt, sugar

For serving
10 sprigs cilantro

PREPARATION

Asparagus

1. Combine ½ cup/100 ml water and the sugar in a saucepan and bring to a boil. Stir in the miso, sake, fish sauce, and soy sauce. Cut 1 inch/2.5 cm off the bottom of each spear. Add the asparagus to the miso sauce mixture and marinate for 3 hours.

Beurre blanc

1. Wash and quarter the tomatoes, then remove the seeds. Slice the quarters into strips and set aside. Cut the butter into cubes and refrigerate.

2. Heat the sake and rice vinegar in a saucepan. Using a whisk, slowly and gradually stir in the cold butter. (During this process, the temperature should always remain between 86 and 104°F/30 and 40°C.)

3. Season the beurre blanc with salt and sugar to taste and add the tomato strips. Remove the sauce from the heat to prevent it from separating.

TO SERVE

Simmer the asparagus and miso sauce in a pan until the asparagus is tender and the sauce is slightly caramelized. Wash the cilantro and shake it dry, then coarsely chop. Divide the asparagus into two bowls and top with the strips of tomato. Pour the beurre blanc sauce over the asparagus, drizzle with a bit of the miso sauce, and garnish with the chopped cilantro.

Bowl: studio1.berlin

ROASTED BEETS
& WILD GARLIC PISTACHIO PESTO

SERVES 2

INGREDIENTS

Roasted beets
1⅓ lb/600 g mixed beets and radishes
Olive oil
Salt, pepper, sugar

Pesto
3½ oz/100 g wild garlic (also known as
   wild leek or ramps)
½ cup/120 ml olive oil
¼ cup/50 g grated Parmesan
2 oz/50 g pistachios, toasted
Grated zest from 1 organic lemon
Salt, pepper, sugar

For serving
1 purple carrot
Apple cider vinegar
Salt, sugar
2 oz/50 g feta cheese

Other
Blender (such as a Vitamix Pro 750)

PREPARATION

Roasted beets

1. Preheat the oven to 400°F/200°C, then line a baking sheet with parchment paper. Wash the beets and radishes and cut them into slices and wedges. Toss the pieces with olive oil until they are thoroughly coated.

2. Spread out the beets and radishes on the baking sheet and roast them for 15 to 20 minutes. Remove them from the oven and season with salt and pepper.

Pesto

1. While the vegetables are roasting, wash the wild garlic and shake it dry. Combine the wild garlic, oil, Parmesan, and pistachios in the blender jar. Add the lemon zest and salt, pepper, and sugar to taste and blend everything into a pesto.

TO SERVE

Peel the carrot and cut into thin spirals. Marinate in vinegar, salt, and sugar. Divide the roasted beets and radishes into two bowls and drizzle with the pesto. Decorate with the carrot spirals and garnish with crumbled feta.

CHILI SIN CARNE

SERVES 2

INGREDIENTS

1 oz/30 g textured vegetable protein (TVP)
4½ oz/130 g red bell pepper
5 oz/150 g eggplant
3½ oz/100 g zucchini
6 oz/170 g tomatoes
Vegetable oil
2 tbsp tomato paste
Grated zest from ¼ organic orange
Salt, pepper, sugar
Red pepper flakes
⅔ cup/150 ml tomato juice
¼ cup/50 ml orange juice

PREPARATION

1. Prepare the textured vegetable protein according to the package instructions.

2. Wash and dice the red bell pepper, eggplant, zucchini, and tomatoes.

3. Heat some oil in a large skillet and brown the textured vegetable protein. Add the bell pepper, eggplant, zucchini, and tomatoes and stir. Stir in the tomato paste and orange zest and season with salt, pepper, sugar, and pepper flakes to taste.

4. Pour in the tomato juice and orange juice and simmer the chili for 5 minutes. Taste and adjust the seasonings as needed.

TO SERVE

Divide the chili into two small casserole dishes or bowls.

Bowl: Staub

COBIA CEVICHE
& TOMATILLO SALAD

SERVES 2

INGREDIENTS

Ceviche
10 oz/300 g cobia fillet (black kingfish
   or lemonfish)
1 organic lime
4 tsp/20 ml olive oil
1 tbsp fish sauce
10 sprigs fresh cilantro
1 chile pepper
Salt, pepper, sugar

Tomato salad
2 green tomatoes
1 tamarillo (tree tomato)
¼ red onion

PREPARATION

Ceviche
1. Rinse the fish in cold water, pat dry, and cut into
   ¾-inch/2-cm cubes. Zest and juice the lime and
   combine with the oil and fish sauce.

2. Wash the cilantro, spin dry, and chop. Wash the pepper,
   cut in half, and slice into thin strips. Stir the cilantro
   and pepper into the lime marinade.

3. Place the fish in the marinade and season with salt,
   pepper, and sugar to taste. Let it "cook" in the marinade
   for at least 5 minutes, allowing the acid to coagulate
   the fish protein.

Tomato salad
1. Wash, quarter, and seed the tomatoes. Set the seeds
   aside. Slice the tomato quarters lengthwise into strips.
   Peel the tamarillo and cut into sections. Peel and thinly
   slice the onion. Mix together the tomato slices, seeds,
   tamarillo, and onion.

TO SERVE

Mix the fish with the tomato salad and arrange
the ceviche in two bowls.

DOLMA & ARUGULA SAUCE

SERVES 2

INGREDIENTS

Dolma
2 globe squash or large tomatoes
¼ cup/40 g bulgur
Salt, pepper
⅓ cup/60 g soft wheat berries
4 tsp pine nuts
¼ cup/60 ml olive oil
1 tbsp tomato paste
1 tbsp pomegranate syrup
2 tbsp lemon juice
Red pepper flakes
Ground cardamom
Ground cumin
Ground cinnamon
¼ pomegranate

Arugula sauce
¼ cup/10 g arugula
6 basil leaves
3 tbsp avocado flesh
¼ cup/50 ml apple juice
Salt, pepper, sugar
1 tbsp lemon juice

Other
Blender (such as a Vitamix Pro 750)

PREPARATION

Dolma
1. Wash the squash, cut off the tops to form a lid, and scoop out the flesh with a spoon and set in a baking dish.

2. Simmer the bulgur in ⅓ cup/80 ml salted water for about 20 minutes. Cook the wheat berries in salted water for about 10 minutes.

3. Preheat the oven to 325°F/170°C. Lightly toast the pine nuts in a skillet with a little of the oil.

4. Combine the bulgur and wheat berries with the remaining oil, tomato paste, syrup, and lemon juice. Season the mixture with salt, pepper, pepper flakes, cardamom, cumin, and cinnamon to taste.

5. Remove the seeds from the pomegranate and fold into the grain mixture. Fill the squash, cover with the squash lids, and bake in the oven for 40 to 50 minutes until done.

Arugula sauce
1. Wash the arugula and basil and pat dry. Combine the herbs, avocado, apple juice, and 3 tbsp water in the blender jar and puree until smooth. Season the sauce with the lemon juice and salt, pepper, and sugar to taste.

TO SERVE

Divide the arugula sauce between two bowls and arrange the dolma on top. The dolma are especially delicious if you let them rest for a day before serving.

MACKEREL, ONION TAPIOCA & SUNCHOKES

SERVES 2

INGREDIENTS

Mackerel
2 whole mackerel
1 cup/300 g coarse sea salt

Tapioca
9 oz/250 g onions
3 tbsp apple juice
4 allspice berries
2 bay leaves
1 tbsp pearl tapioca
1 tbsp apple cider vinegar
Salt, pepper, sugar

Sunchokes
5 oz/160 g sunchokes
2 tbsp vegetable oil
Salt, pepper, sugar
Ground cinnamon

For serving
¼ red onion
Sprouts or microgreens

PREPARATION

Mackerel
1. Clean and fillet the mackerel. Lay the fillets on the salt, flesh side down. Cool in the fridge and allow to marinate for 2½ hours.

Tapioca
1. Preheat the oven to 425°F/220°C. Line a baking sheet with parchment paper. Peel the onions, coarsely chop, place on the baking sheet, and bake for about 25 minutes, or until golden brown. Then combine with 1½ cups/400 ml water, the apple juice, allspice, and bay leaves in a saucepan and bring to a boil. Simmer for 45 minutes.

2. Strain the broth through a sieve and bring to a boil again. Stir in the tapioca and simmer until it turns translucent. Remove from the stove, add the vinegar, and season with salt, pepper, and sugar to taste.

Sunchokes
1. Peel the sunchokes and cut into ¼-inch/6-mm slices. Heat the oil in a skillet and lightly sauté the slices on both sides. Season with salt, pepper, sugar, and cinnamon to taste.

TO SERVE

Rinse off the mackerel and cut each fillet into three pieces. Peel the red onion and cut into thin strips. Divide the onion tapioca between two bowls and arrange the mackerel and sautéed sunchokes on top. Sprinkle with onion strips and sprouts.

Bowl: studio1.berlin

SCALLOP CARPACCIO, CAULIFLOWER & RASPBERRIES

SERVES 2

INGREDIENTS

Cauliflower
8 oz/250 g cauliflower
½ cup/100 g coconut milk
1 tsp fish sauce
Salt, sugar
1 tsp sesame oil
2 tbsp teriyaki sauce

Carpaccio
6 scallops, removed from the shells
2 tbsp olive oil
Salt
Grated zest from ½ organic lemon

For serving
8 raspberries

Other
Culinary torch

PREPARATION

Cauliflower
1. Wash the cauliflower. Divide half of it into small florets and slice the rest ¼ inch/5 mm thick.

2. Combine the coconut milk, fish sauce, and salt and sugar to taste in a saucepan and bring to a boil. Add the cauliflower slices and cook over low heat for 5 to 10 minutes until tender.

3. Heat the sesame oil in a skillet and sauté the florets. Add the teriyaki sauce and continue cooking for another minute.

Carpaccio
1. Rinse the scallops in cold water, pat dry, and cut into slices, about ⅛ inch/4 mm thick. Sear the scallop slices with the culinary torch. Brush them with oil and sprinkle with salt and lemon zest to taste.

TO SERVE

Wash the raspberries and cut them in half. Layer the cauliflower and scallop slices in two bowls. Pour some of the coconut sauce over them and arrange the cauliflower florets and raspberries on the carpaccio.

SALMON
& SAKE-MARINATED CUCUMBER

SERVES 2

INGREDIENTS

Cucumber
7 oz/200 g cucumber
1 tbsp butter
3 tbsp sake (Japanese rice wine)
4 tsp Japanese rice vinegar
Salt, sugar

Salmon
8 oz/250 g skin-on salmon fillet
2 tbsp vegetable oil
Salt
1 scallion
½ sheet nori
1 tbsp unagi sauce (eel sauce,
   available at Asian markets)

For serving
1 tbsp sesame oil

PREPARATION

Cucumber
1. Wash the cucumber, cut into quarters lengthwise,
   and remove the seeds. Heat the butter in a saucepan and
   lightly sauté the cucumber quarters. Add the sake and
   rice vinegar and season with salt and sugar to taste.
   Simmer the cucumber for 1 minute and set aside.

Salmon
1. Rinse the salmon, pat dry, and divide into two fillets.
   Heat the oil in a skillet and fry the fillets, skin side down,
   over medium heat until crispy. Turn the fish over,
   remove from the heat, and season with salt.

2. Trim the scallion, rinse, and cut into thin rings. Slice the nori
   into strips. Mix the two together. Drizzle the unagi sauce
   over the salmon and sprinkle with the scallion-nori mixture.

TO SERVE

Reheat the cucumber and arrange with the broth in
two bowls. Place the salmon on top and drizzle with
sesame oil.

RASPBERRY GAZPACHO & OLIVE STICKS

SERVES 2

INGREDIENTS

Gazpacho
5 oz/150 g tomatoes
3½ oz/100 g red bell pepper
1 oz/30 g celery
3 oz/80 g cucumber
1 shallot
½ garlic clove
1 cup/150 g raspberries
7 tbsp raspberry vinegar
Salt, pepper, sugar
⅞ cup/200 ml olive oil

Olive sticks
2 oz/50 g black olives
2 sprigs thyme
½ garlic clove
⅓ oz/10 g sun-dried tomatoes
3 tbsp olive oil
Grated zest from ½ organic lemon
Salt, pepper
1 sheet frozen puff pastry (2½ oz/70 g)
1 oz/20 g freshly grated Parmesan

For serving
Olive oil
Basil leaves

Other
Blender (such as a Vitamix Pro 750)

PREPARATION

Gazpacho
1. Wash and trim the tomatoes, bell pepper, and celery. Peel the cucumber, shallot, and garlic. Coarsely chop everything.

2. Combine the vegetables, raspberries, and vinegar in the blender jar and puree until creamy. Slowly blend in the oil. Season with salt, pepper, and sugar to taste and then strain through a fine sieve. Refrigerate the soup until ready to serve.

Olive sticks
1. Preheat the oven to 425°F/220°C, then line a baking sheet with parchment paper. Wash the thyme and shake dry.

2. Pit and finely chop the olives. Finely chop the thyme, garlic, and sun-dried tomatoes. Mix everything with the oil and the lemon zest and season with salt and pepper to taste.

3. Roll the puff pastry dough out very thinly (2 mm). Spread the olive mixture evenly over the puff pastry. Fold the dough lengthwise, press down carefully, and cut lengthwise into ⅜-inch/1-cm-wide strips.

4. Twist each strip from both sides, then sprinkle with the Parmesan and place on the baking sheet. Repeat with the remaining strips. Bake in the oven until golden, 5 to 7 minutes.

TO SERVE

Ladle the soup into two bowls, drizzle with a bit of olive oil, and decorate with basil leaves. Serve with the olive sticks.

Bowl: Royal Copenhagen

OVEN-DRIED CANTALOUPE, GOAT CHEESE ESPUMA & SERRANO HAM

SERVES 2

INGREDIENTS

Cantaloupe
1 cantaloupe
Sea salt, pepper

Goat cheese espuma
1½ tsp unflavored gelatin
½ cup/120 ml milk
4 oz/125 g goat cheese
1 tbsp honey
Salt

For serving
Walnut oil
Toasted pistachios
Sprouts
Pepper
8 slices serrano ham

Other
Blender (such as a Vitamix Pro 750)
Siphon (cream whipper)
N2O cartridge

PREPARATION

Cantaloupe

1. Preheat the oven to 210°F/100°C. Line a baking sheet with parchment paper. Peel the cantaloupe, cut it in half and scoop out the seeds. Cut the melon halves into ¼-inch/6-mm slices, place on the baking sheet, and season with salt and pepper to taste.

2. Allow the melon slices to dry in the oven for 1 hour and 30 minutes, opening the oven door every 10 minutes to allow the moisture to escape.

Goat cheese espuma

1. Soak the gelatin in ¼ cup/60 ml of the milk to soften. Meanwhile, puree the remaining milk, the cheese, honey, and salt to taste in the blender.

2. Remove some of the cheese mixture, heat on the stove, and dissolve the gelatin in the mixture. Then fold the gelatin mixture into the rest of the puree and adjust the seasonings.

3. Place everything in the siphon and screw on the N2O cartridge. Refrigerate the siphon until ready to serve.

TO SERVE

Roll up the melon slices and arrange in a circular pattern in two bowls. Put two slices of serrano ham in the middle and squirt the goat cheese espuma on top. Drizzle with a bit of walnut oil, sprinkle with pistachios and sprouts, and season with freshly ground pepper. Add the rest of the serrano ham.

Bowl: studio1.berlin

CHILLED CUCUMBER SOUP, ALOE VERA & KATAIFI

SERVES 2

INGREDIENTS

Chilled soup
1 cucumber
2 sprigs dill
5 oz/150 g plain yogurt (or soy yogurt
  for a vegan alternative)
2 tbsp aloe vera juice
  (from the aloe vera in syrup)
Grated zest from ½ organic lemon
4 tsp gin
Salt, pepper, sugar

Kataifi sticks
1½ oz/40 g kataifi (shredded phyllo
  dough; available at Turkish markets
  or the frozen foods section of larger
  supermarkets)
2 sprigs dill
2 tbsp unsalted butter
Sea salt flakes

For serving
1 sprig dill
2 oz/60 g aloe vera in syrup
  (available at Asian markets)

Other
Blender (such as a Vitamix Pro 750)

PREPARATION

Chilled soup
1. Wash the cucumber and cut into chunks, then wash
   and shake dry the dill. Combine the cucumber, dill,
   yogurt, aloe vera juice, lemon zest, gin, and salt, pepper,
   and sugar to taste in the blender jar, then puree
   until creamy. Adjust the seasonings in the soup as needed
   and refrigerate until ready to serve.

Kataifi sticks
1. Preheat the oven to 400°F/200°C, then line a baking sheet
   with parchment paper. Form the kataifi into two strands
   about 8 inches/20 cm in length and roughly the thickness
   of a finger and place them on the baking sheet.

2. Wash the dill, shake dry, and pinch off the tips.
   Sprinkle the dill on the kataifi and twist the strands together.
   Melt the butter and drizzle over the sticks. Lightly salt
   the sticks and bake in the oven for 5 minutes until golden.

TO SERVE

Wash the dill, shake dry, then pinch off the tips.
Divide the aloe vera into two bowls. Pour the chilled soup
over the aloe vera, then sprinkle with dill and serve
with the kataifi sticks.

Bowl: studio1.berlin

SWEET
BOWLS

KÜNEFE & WILD BERRY FROZEN YOGURT

SERVES 4

INGREDIENTS

Frozen yogurt
14 oz/400 g frozen berries
½ cup/60 g powdered sugar
⅔ cup/150 g plain yogurt
2 tsp Grand Marnier
4 tsp lemon juice
Grated zest from ½ organic lemon
Salt

Künefe
6 oz/160 g kataifi (shredded phyllo
   dough; available at Turkish markets
   or the frozen foods section of
   larger supermarkets)
1 buffalo mozzarella (4 oz/125 g)
6 tbsp unsalted butter

Syrup
7 tbsp sugar
⅓ cup/80 ml orange juice
Grated zest from ½ organic orange
Salt, cinnamon

For serving
Toasted pistachios

Other
Blender (such as a Vitamix Pro 750)
4 small tart pans (3½ inch/9 cm
   in diameter)

PREPARATION

Frozen yogurt
1. Combine the berries, powdered sugar, yogurt, Grand Marnier, lemon juice, lemon zest, and salt to taste in the blender and puree until smooth. Pour the yogurt mixture into a prechilled bowl and freeze until ready to serve.

Künefe
1. Preheat the oven to 375°F/190°C. Pull apart the kataifi dough and cut into pieces about ¾ inch/2 cm in length. Take half of the dough and press it into the tart pans.

2. Cut the mozzarella into four slices and place one slice in the center of the dough in each pan. Sprinkle the remaining dough over the cheese and press down evenly.

3. Melt the butter and drizzle over the dough. Place the künefe in the oven and bake for 30 minutes until golden brown and crispy. Remove them from the oven.

Syrup
1. While the künefe are baking, combine the sugar, orange juice, orange zest, salt, and cinnamon to taste in a saucepan and bring to a boil.

2. Let the syrup cool somewhat, then drizzle over the baked künefe. Let soak for about 5 minutes before removing the künefe from the tart pans.

TO SERVE

Briefly reheat the künefe in the oven, then arrange in four bowls. Add a scoop of frozen yogurt to each and sprinkle with pistachios.

GUAVA PORRIDGE & GRAPEFRUIT

SERVES 2

INGREDIENTS

Porridge
1 cup/250 ml guava juice
¼ cup/50 ml passion fruit juice
Grated zest from ¼ organic orange
¼ vanilla bean
2 tbsp sugar
Salt
1¼ cups/100 g quick rolled oats
3½ oz/100 g soy creamer
   (such as Organic Valley)

Topping
1 red grapefruit
2 dates
1 tbsp chia seeds

PREPARATION

Porridge
1. In a saucepan, combine the guava juice, passion fruit juice, orange zest, vanilla bean, sugar, and salt to taste and bring to a boil.

2. Stir in the oats and simmer for 1 minute. Pour in the soy creamer and stir. Remove the pot from the heat and let the porridge stand for 5 minutes.

Topping
1. Peel the grapefruit, taking care to remove the white pith as well. Use a knife to carefully separate the grapefruit segments from between the membranes.

2. Remove the pits from the dates, then cut lengthwise into fine strips.

TO SERVE

Divide the porridge into two bowls. Arrange the grapefruit segments and the date strips on top and sprinkle with chia seeds.

BERRY TAPIOCA PUDDING & VANILLA SAUCE

SERVES 2

INGREDIENTS

Tapioca pudding
2 cups/450 ml cherry juice
½ cup/100 ml red wine
Grated zest of ½ organic orange
¼ vanilla bean
Pinch ground cinnamon
Salt
2 oz/60 g small pearl tapioca
11 oz/300 g frozen mixed berries
2½ tbsp sugar

Vanilla sauce
½ cup/125 ml heavy cream
2 large egg yolks
5 tsp sugar
¼ vanilla bean
Salt

For serving
1 handful of fresh berries

PREPARATION

Tapioca pudding

1. In a saucepan, combine the juice, wine, orange zest, vanilla bean, cinnamon, and salt to taste, and bring the mixture to a boil.

2. Stir in the tapioca and simmer for 5 minutes. Reduce the heat to the lowest setting and let the tapioca steep until the pearls become translucent, stirring regularly. Discard the vanilla bean.

3. Stir in the berries and the sugar, then chill the tapioca pudding for about 1 hour.

Vanilla sauce

1. For the water bath, bring some water to a boil in a large saucepan. Whisk together the cream, egg yolks, sugar, vanilla bean, and salt in a stainless-steel bowl.

2. Place the bowl over the hot water bath and, while stirring constantly, heat the cream mixture until it thickens to a creamy consistency. Remove the sauce from the water bath and discard the vanilla bean. Chill for 30 minutes.

TO SERVE

Wash the berries and pat them dry. Divide the tapioca pudding into two bowls, pour the vanilla sauce over the pudding, and garnish with the fresh berries.

SPICED FRENCH TOAST

SERVES 3

INGREDIENTS

Bacon
Vegetable oil
9 slices bacon

Toast
¼ cup/60 ml milk
¼ cup/60 ml heavy cream
2 large eggs
2½ tsp sugar
1 tsp stollen spices* (see note)
Grated zest from ½ organic lemon
Salt
9 slices white sandwich bread
  (¾ in/2 cm thick)
Vegetable oil
1 tsp unsalted butter

For serving
Powdered sugar
Maple syrup

*To make a blend of stollen spices,
mix together equal parts of
the following spices (ground): allspice,
anise seed, cardamom, cinnamon,
cloves, coriander, and vanilla powder.
Reserve the unused portion for
future use.

PREPARATION

Bacon
1. Heat some oil in a skillet, add the bacon, and fry
   until crispy. Drain the bacon on a paper towel.

Toast
1. Whisk together the milk, cream, eggs, sugar, spices,
   lemon zest, and salt to taste.

2. One by one, dip the bread slices into the egg mixture,
   turning the slices over so the bread can fully absorb
   the liquid.

3. Heat some oil in a large skillet and fry the bread slices
   on both sides until golden brown. Add the butter last.

TO SERVE

Arrange the slices of French toast with the bacon
in three bowls. Dust with powdered sugar and
drizzle with maple syrup.

MANGO SPRING ROLLS & SPICED COFFEE DIP

SERVES 2

INGREDIENTS

Spring rolls
4 oz/120 g mango
¾ cup/90 g crème fraîche
2 oz/60 g white chocolate
2½ tsp coconut sugar
Grated zest from ½ organic lime
Salt
1 medium egg white
6 spring roll wrappers
Vegetable oil

Dip
9 oz/250 g mango
⅓ cup/40 g crème fraîche
2 tbsp orange juice
1 tsp instant coffee powder
¼ tsp ground cinnamon

Other
Blender (such as a Vitamix Pro 750)

PREPARATION

Spring rolls
1. Peel the mango, slice the flesh away from the seed, and then cut the mango into ¼-inch/6-mm cubes. Combine the crème fraîche and chocolate in a saucepan and melt over low heat while stirring. Add the mango cubes, coconut sugar, lime zest, and salt to taste.

2. Stir the egg white until smooth. Cut the spring roll wrappers in half and add 2 teaspoons of the mango mixture to the lower half of each wrapper. Fold in the sides and, starting at the bottom, roll the wrappers up. Lightly brush the upper end of the wrapper with egg white to seal the rolls.

3. Add a generous amount of oil to a pot and heat it to 350°F/180°C. Fry the spring rolls in the hot oil in batches until golden brown, then drain them on paper towels.

Dip
1. Peel the mango and slice the flesh away from the seed. Combine the mango with the crème fraîche, orange juice, coffee powder, and cinnamon in the blender jar and puree until creamy. Adjust the seasonings to taste.

TO SERVE

Arrange the spring rolls in two bowls and enjoy hot with the dip.

EGG LIQUEUR
& CHOCOLATE MARSHMALLOWS

SERVES 4

INGREDIENTS

Egg liqueur
4 large egg yolks
¼ cup/60 ml heavy cream
3 tbsp sugar
⅔ cup/150 ml sweetened condensed milk
⅓ cup/80 ml rum
3 tbsp brandy

PREPARATION

Egg liqueur

1. For the water bath, bring some water to a boil in a large saucepan. Whisk together the egg yolks, cream, sugar, and condensed milk in a stainless-steel bowl.

2. Place the bowl over the hot water bath and, while stirring constantly, heat the egg yolk mixture to a temperature of 155°F/70°C until it thickens to a creamy consistency. To test whether it is done, dip a wooden spoon into the mixture and blow on it. If the cream on the spoon ripples into a rose shape, it means the cream has thickened perfectly.

3. Stir the rum and the brandy into the egg yolk mixture. Remove the bowl from the water bath, set it in a bowl of ice water and let it cool.

4. Strain the egg liqueur through a fine sieve, then pour it into bottles or an airtight container and store in the refrigerator.

Marshmallows
5 sheets silver gelatin
1½ oz/40 g dark chocolate
2 large egg whites
⅓ cup/70 g sugar
2 tsp Licor 43

Marshmallows

1. Soak the gelatin in cold water for 5 minutes. Coarsely chop the chocolate and melt in a bowl over the hot water bath.

2. Whip the egg whites in a stand mixer.

3. Bring the sugar and 3 tbsp water to a boil in a saucepan, then heat to 250°F/119°C. Use a candy thermometer to check the temperature, or dip a fork into the syrup and gently blow through the tines. If bubbles form, the syrup is hot enough.

4. While the mixer is running, drizzle the hot syrup into the beaten egg whites. Continue to beat until the egg whites have cooled.

5. Gently squeeze the water from the gelatin, then dissolve the gelatin with the Licor 43 in a small saucepan. Gently stir the mixture into the beaten egg whites. Last, fold in the melted chocolate.

6. Line a container with plastic wrap, then pour in the chocolate mixture and place in the refrigerator for about 1 hour to set.

TO SERVE

Divide the egg liqueur into four bowls or cups.
Cut the marshmallow into cubes and arrange on top.

SPICED SQUASH
& GREEK FROZEN YOGURT

SERVES 4

INGREDIENTS

Yogurt
1 cup/300 g plain Greek yogurt
3½ tbsp heavy cream
3 tbsp honey
1 tbsp lemon juice
Salt

Spiced squash
7 oz/200 g butternut squash
¼ cup/50 g sugar
1 tsp unsalted butter
¼ cup/50 ml orange juice
Grated zest from ¼ organic orange
¼ vanilla bean
3 cardamom pods
1 star anise pod
1 cinnamon stick
Salt
3½ tbsp crème fraîche

For serving
2 tbsp pumpkin seed oil
¼ cup/35 g pumpkin seeds (pepitas)
Salt

Other
Ice cube tray
Blender (such as a Vitamix Pro 750)

PREPARATION

Yogurt
1. Spoon the yogurt into the ice cube tray and place it in the freezer overnight.

2. The next day, remove the yogurt cubes from the tray and put them in the blender jar along with the cream, honey, lemon juice, and salt to taste. Puree for about 1 minute until creamy. Pour the frozen puree into a bowl and place it in the freezer for 30 minutes.

Spiced squash
1. Peel the butternut squash and cut into ⅜-inch/1-cm dice. Heat the sugar and 3 tbsp water in a saucepan and stir until caramelized. Add the butter and stir until melted.

2. Stir in the cubes of butternut squash and let them caramelize. Add the orange juice, orange zest, vanilla bean, cardamom, star anise, cinnamon, and salt to taste.

3. Simmer the squash over low heat until tender. Stir in the crème fraîche and remove the squash from the heat.

TO SERVE

Heat the pumpkin seed oil in a skillet and sauté the pumpkin seeds, adding salt to taste. Arrange the spiced squash in four bowls and top with a large scoop of the frozen yogurt. Sprinkle with the pumpkin seeds.

Bowl: studio1.berlin

WHEAT BEER
PRETZEL BREAD PUDDING

SERVES 3

INGREDIENTS

Bread pudding
5½ oz/160 g soft pretzels
⅞ cup/200 ml wheat beer
Grated zest from ¼ organic orange
½ banana

Royale custard
⅔ cup/150 ml beer
⅔ cup/150 ml heavy cream
¼ cup/45 g sugar
1 large egg
3 large egg yolks
1 tsp Licor 43
Grated zest from ¼ organic orange
Salt

For serving
Powdered sugar

PREPARATION

Bread pudding
1. Cut the pretzels into large cubes. Mix the cubes with the beer and orange zest and let soak for 10 minutes.

2. In the meantime, peel the banana and cut into ¼-inch/6-mm-thick slices. Arrange the banana slices on the bottom of a large ovensafe bowl.

3. Drain the pretzel cubes in a sieve and then spoon onto the bananas.

Royale custard
1. Preheat the oven to 250°F/120°C. While the oven heats, carefully slide a roasting pan onto the center oven rack and pour in ¾ inch/2 cm very hot water.

2. Whisk together the beer, cream, sugar, egg, egg yolks, Licor 43, orange zest, and salt to taste. Carefully pour the beer and cream mixture over the pretzel cubes in the bowl.

3. Carefully place the bowl in the hot water bath and bake the pudding for 40 to 50 minutes. To check whether the pudding is done, gently shake the tray. If the pudding no longer jiggles, it is fully cooked.

TO SERVE

Remove the bowl of bread pudding from the oven and let it cool slightly. Dust with powdered sugar and serve either warm or cold.

SOUR CREAM SCHMARRN & BLUEBERRY PEARS

SERVES 3

INGREDIENTS

Sour cream schmarrn
5 medium eggs
9 oz/250 g sour cream
1 cup/250 ml heavy cream
1½ cups/200 g all-purpose flour
2 tbsp rum
Pulp from ½ vanilla bean
Grated zest from ½ organic lemon
Ground cinnamon
Salt
½ cup/100 g sugar
Vegetable oil
1½ oz/50 g slivered almonds, toasted
1½ oz/50 g raisins
Pats of unsalted butter
Powdered sugar

Blueberry pears
1 pear
5 oz/150 g blueberries
3 tbsp sugar
3 tbsp unsalted butter
3½ oz/100 ml cherry juice
1 tsp grated fresh ginger
Grated zest from ¼ organic orange
Salt, ground cinnamon

TO SERVE

Arrange the schmarrn and fruit in three
bowls and dust with powdered sugar.

PREPARATION

Sour cream schmarrn
1. Preheat the oven to 425°F/220°C. Separate four eggs. Beat the egg yolks along with the remaining whole egg, sour cream, cream, flour, rum, vanilla, lemon zest, cinnamon, and salt to taste until the mixture is smooth.

2. Whip the egg whites with the sugar until stiff, then gently fold into the batter.

3. Heat some vegetable oil in one large or two smaller ovensafe skillets. Pour in the batter and sprinkle with the almonds and raisins.

4. Slide the pan into the oven and bake the schmarrn for about 15 minutes.

5. Remove the schmarrn and place the skillet on a burner over medium heat.

6. Flip the schmarrn and, using two spoons, tear it into pieces. Add a few pats of butter, dust with powdered sugar, and let the pieces caramelize.

Blueberry pears
1. While the schmarrn is baking, peel the pear, quarter it, and remove the core before slicing. Sort the berries, then wash and pat dry.

2. Melt the sugar in a saucepan and cook until golden brown, then stir in the butter. Add the pear, berries, cherry juice, orange zest, and salt and cinnamon to taste. Simmer over medium heat for 5 minutes until it has a creamy consistency.

Bowl: Royal Copenhagen

PAVLOVA, SALTED CREAM & BALSAMIC BERRIES

SERVES 3

INGREDIENTS

Meringue shells
3 large egg whites
¾ cup/150 g sugar
Salt

Salted cream
½ cup/125 ml heavy cream
1 tbsp sugar
Pulp from ¼ vanilla bean
Salt

Balsamic berries
⅓ cup/60 g blueberries
2 tbsp sugar
2 tsp balsamic vinegar
Grated zest from ½ organic orange
2 tbsp orange juice
Salt

For serving
1 handful mixed berries

PREPARATION

Meringue shells
1. Preheat the oven to 250°F/120°C, then line a baking sheet with parchment paper. Combine the egg whites with the sugar and a pinch of salt and whip until stiff.

2. Place one large tablespoon of meringue on the baking sheet and use the back of the spoon to form a hollow in the middle. Repeat twice to make three meringue shells.

3. Bake the meringue shells for about 1 hour. The meringues should be crispy on the outside and still soft on the inside. Remove from the oven and let cool.

Salted cream
1. Combine the cream with the sugar, vanilla pulp, and salt to taste and whip until stiff.

Balsamic berries
1. Sort and wash the berries, then pat dry. Melt the sugar in a saucepan and cook until golden brown, then stir in the balsamic vinegar.

2. Add the berries, orange zest and juice, and salt to taste and cook until the mixture reduces slightly.

TO SERVE

Sort the berries, wash, and pat dry. Fill the meringue shells with a bit of cream and a few berries, then spoon some balsamic berries on top.

MISO CREAM, SAKE PEARS & CILANTRO STREUSEL

SERVES 3

INGREDIENTS

Miso cream
⅔ cup/150 ml milk
⅔ cup/150 g heavy cream
3 oz/75 g white chocolate
2 tbsp wheat starch (or cornstarch)
1½ tbsp sugar
1½ tbsp miso
1 medium egg yolk
2 tsp sake (Japanese rice wine)
2 tsp unsalted butter
Salt

Sake pears
1 pear
2½ tbsp sake (Japanese rice wine)
5 tsp sugar
2 tsp lime juice
Grated zest from ¼ organic lime
Salt

PREPARATION

Miso cream
1. In a saucepan, whisk together the milk, cream, white chocolate, starch, sugar, miso, egg yolk, sake, butter, and salt to taste.

2. Bring the mixture to a boil, stirring constantly, and cook until it thickens to a creamy consistency. Cover the cream and set it in the refrigerator to chill until ready to serve.

Sake pears
1. Peel and quarter the pear, remove the core, and cut it into slices.

2. Combine the sake, sugar, lime juice and zest, salt to taste, and ⅓ cup/80 ml water in a saucepan and bring to a boil. Add the pear slices and simmer for 2 minutes. Remove the pot from the heat and let the pears steep until ready to serve.

Cilantro streusel
5 sprigs cilantro
¼ cup/25 g cashews
3 tbsp unsalted butter
2½ tbsp sugar
½ cup/60 g flour
Grated zest from ¼ organic lime
Salt

For serving
⅓ cup/30 g white chocolate shavings

Cilantro streusel

1. Wash the cilantro and shake dry. Pinch off the leaves and chop them. Coarsely chop the cashews.

2. Mix together the butter and sugar, then knead in the flour. Add the cashews, lime zest, and salt to taste and continue kneading. Wrap the dough in plastic wrap and chill for 30 minutes.

3. Preheat the oven to 375°F/190°C and line a baking sheet with parchment paper. Pinch coarse pieces of streusel off the chilled dough, spread out on the baking sheet, then bake in the oven for 7 to 10 minutes, or until golden.

TO SERVE

Whisk the cold miso cream until smooth and spoon into three bowls. Top with the sake pear slices and cilantro streusel, then sprinkle with shavings of white chocolate.

CHERRY MERINGUE

SERVES 4

INGREDIENTS

Coconut sponge cake
3 large eggs
⅓ cup/70 g coconut sugar
⅔ cup/50 g shredded coconut
½ cup/50 g almond flour
¼ cup/30 g all-purpose flour
Salt

Cherry compote
½ cup/125 ml cherry juice
⅓ cup/60 g sugar
1 tbsp cornstarch
½ vanilla bean
Grated zest from ¼ organic orange
Salt
9 oz/250 g frozen cherries

Meringue
2 large egg whites
6½ tbsp sugar
Salt

For serving
⅓ cup/120 g plain Greek yogurt
Grated zest from ½ organic orange

Other
Culinary torch

PREPARATION

Coconut sponge cake
1. Preheat the oven to 375°F/190°C, then line a baking sheet with parchment paper. Separate the eggs. Beat the egg yolks and the egg whites separately, then gently fold them together. In sequence, gently fold in the coconut sugar, shredded coconut, almond flour, all-purpose flour, and salt to taste.

2. Spread the batter on the baking sheet to a depth of ¾ inch/2 cm. Bake for 20 minutes until golden. Remove and let cool.

Cherry compote
1. Combine the cherry juice, sugar, starch, vanilla bean, orange zest, and salt in a saucepan. Bring the mixture to a boil, stirring constantly, until it thickens. Stir in the cherries and let thaw for 2 minutes, then remove the compote from the heat.

Meringue
1. Combine the egg whites with the sugar and one pinch of salt and whip until stiff, forming a creamy meringue.

TO SERVE

Divide the sponge cake into pieces and arrange in four bowls. Spoon the compote and the yogurt over the sponge cake. Using two spoons, carefully add one meringue cloud to the top of each serving. Use the culinary torch to lightly brown the meringue. Sprinkle with orange zest.

HAY PANNA COTTA & APRICOTS

SERVES 3

INGREDIENTS

Hay panna cotta
¼ oz/5 g organic hay (about 1 handful)
1¼ cups/295 ml heavy cream
½ cup/100 ml milk
  (plus ½ cup/100 ml for the gelatin)
3 tbsp sugar
Salt
2¼ tsp unflavored gelatin

Apricots
3 apricots
1 tbsp sugar
1 tsp unsalted butter
1 tbsp sunflower seeds
3 tbsp apricot juice
1 tbsp lemon juice
Grated zest from ½ organic lemon
Salt

PREPARATION

Hay panna cotta
1. Preheat the oven to 375°F/190°C, then line a baking sheet with parchment paper. Spread the hay out on the baking sheet and toast in the oven for about 3 minutes until it begins to take on color.

2. Combine the hay, cream, milk, sugar, and salt to taste in a saucepan and heat until it simmers. Remove the cream from the heat and let it sit for 30 minutes.

3. Soak the gelatin in the milk to soften. Strain the cream mixture through a sieve and reheat slightly. Stir the gelatin-milk mixture into the warm cream mixture to dissolve. Pour the panna cotta into three bowls and refrigerate for 2 hours.

Apricots
1. Wash the apricots, slice in half, and remove the pits. Chop the apricot halves.

2. Melt the sugar in a small skillet and cook until golden brown. Add the butter and sunflower seeds and toast them in the caramel. Add the apricots, apricot juice, lemon juice, lemon zest, and salt to taste, toss briefly, and remove from the heat.

TO SERVE

Spoon the caramelized apricots onto the panna cotta.

VANILLA PASTA & PASSION FRUIT

SERVES 2

INGREDIENTS

1⅔ cups/400 ml milk
7 tbsp heavy cream
½ vanilla bean
2 tsp Licor 43
Salt
1 cup/120 g small pasta shells
  or other short pasta
2 oz/50 g white chocolate

For serving
1 passion fruit
1 handful blueberries
3 tbsp white chocolate shavings

PREPARATION

1. Combine the milk, cream, vanilla bean, Licor 43, and salt to taste in a pot and bring the mixture to a boil.

2. Add the pasta and, simmer over low heat, stirring occasionally, until the pasta is al dente.

3. Break the white chocolate into small pieces and add to the pasta, stirring until melted. Taste the pasta and season with salt to taste if necessary.

TO SERVE

Slice the passion fruit in half and scoop out the fruit. Sort through the blueberries, then wash and pat dry. Arrange the pasta in two bowls. Top with the passion fruit, berries, and white chocolate shavings.

Bowl: ASA

MATCHA BIRCHER MUESLI

SERVES 3

INGREDIENTS

2 oz/50 g banana
9 oz/250 g green apple
½ organic lime
2 sprigs mint
1 cup/250 g coconut yogurt
½ cup/100 ml coconut milk
1 cup/80 g rolled oats
½ cup/50 g roasted cashews
2½ tbsp honey
1 tsp matcha powder
Salt

To serve
2 oz/60 g cucumber
3½ oz/100 g green apple

PREPARATION

1. Peel the banana and mash with a fork. Wash and core the apple, then finely grate.

2. Grate the zest from the lime and then juice the lime. Wash the mint and shake dry. Pick the mint leaves off the stems and finely slice them.

3. In a bowl, combine the fruit, the lime zest and juice, mint, coconut yogurt, coconut milk, oats, cashews, honey, matcha powder, and salt to taste. Adjust the seasonings of the muesli as desired and place in the refrigerator to soak overnight.

TO SERVE

Wash the cucumber and cut into thin slices. Wash and core the apple, then cut into matchsticks. Spoon the muesli into three bowls and top each portion with some sliced cucumber and apple.

Bowl: ASA

RICE PUDDING
& BUTTER COOKIE SNOW

SERVES 2

INGREDIENTS

Butter cookie snow
2½ oz/70 g butter cookies
½ cup/125 g unsalted butter
2 tbsp brown sugar
Salt

Rice pudding
2 tsp unsalted butter
½ cup/100 g short-grain rice
2 tsp Licor 43
2⅓ cups/550 ml milk
Grated zest from ½ organic lemon
   or more to taste
½ vanilla bean or more to taste
Salt
5 tsp sugar

Other
Small rectangular baking pan
   (about 5 by 3½ inches/13 by 9 cm)

PREPARATION

Butter cookie snow
1. Crush the cookies into crumbs. Melt the butter in a saucepan and cook until it browns. Line a sieve with a paper towel, then pour the browned butter through the sieve into a bowl.

2. Mix the cookie crumbs and the sugar into the butter and add salt to taste.

3. Line the baking pan with plastic wrap. Scrape the crumb mixture into the lined pan and press down firmly. Cover the pan, then place in freezer and let it sit for 1 hour.

Rice pudding
1. Melt the butter in a saucepan, then add the rice and sauté lightly. Add the Licor 43 and then pour in the milk.

2. Add the lemon zest, vanilla bean, and salt to taste, then simmer the rice over low heat for about 25 minutes, stirring occasionally.

3. Stir in the sugar and adjust the seasonings of the rice pudding to taste.

TO SERVE

Remove the vanilla bean and divide the rice pudding into two bowls. Remove the frozen block of cookie crumbs from the pan and grate over the warm rice pudding.

RHUBARB BLOODY MARY BOWL

SERVES 3

INGREDIENTS

Rhubarb snow
10 oz/280 g rhubarb
3½ oz/100 ml apple juice
⅓ cup/70 g sugar
¼ vanilla bean
Grated zest from ¼ organic lemon
Salt
3 tbsp plain yogurt
3½ oz/100 g heavy cream, whipped

Rhubarb compote
4 oz/125 g rhubarb
1 oz/20 g frozen raspberries
5 tsp sugar
2 tsp Grand Marnier
2 tsp Campari
¼ vanilla bean
1 strip organic orange peel
1 strip organic lemon peel
Salt

PREPARATION

Rhubarb snow

1. Wash and peel the rhubarb and save the peelings for the stock. Coarsely chop the rhubarb.

2. Combine the chopped rhubarb, apple juice, sugar, vanilla bean, lemon zest, and salt to taste in a saucepan. Bring to a boil and then reduce the heat, allowing the mixture to simmer uncovered until the rhubarb is tender. Remove the vanilla bean, then pour the mixture into the blender jar and puree. Pour the puree into a bowl and let cool.

3. Gently fold the yogurt and the whipped cream into the cold puree. Scoop the mixture into a small container and place it in the freezer overnight.

4. The next day, once the mixture has frozen to a firm consistency, use a fork to scrape off frozen rhubarb crystals into a chilled bowl, creating ice shavings that look like snow. Store the rhubarb snow in the freezer.

Rhubarb compote

1. Preheat the oven to 375°F/190°C. Wash and peel the rhubarb and save the peelings for the stock. Cut the rhubarb into pieces about 2½ inches/7 cm in length.

2. Combine the rhubarb, raspberries, sugar, Grand Marnier, Campari, vanilla bean, orange and lemon peel, and salt to taste in a casserole dish. Cover with aluminum foil and bake for about 15 minutes.

3. Remove the pan from the oven and put it in the fridge to immediately halt the cooking process.

Raspberry vodka stock
1⅜ cups/330 ml apple juice
4 oz/120 g frozen raspberries
2½ tbsp sugar
¼ vanilla bean
Grated zest from ¼ organic orange
Salt
1½ tsp unflavored gelatin
3 tbsp vodka

For serving
1 celery stalk
6 strawberries

Other
Blender (such as a Vitamix Pro 750)

Raspberry vodka stock

1. Combine 1 cup/240 ml of the apple juice, the raspberries, sugar, vanilla bean, orange zest, salt to taste, and the rhubarb peelings in a saucepan. Bring to a boil and simmer over low heat for about 5 minutes.

2. Remove the stock from the heat, cover, and let cool.

3. Soak the gelatin in the remaining ⅜ cup/90 ml apple juice in a medium bowl to soften. Pour the stock through a sieve and reheat the stock again slightly.

4. Pour some of the warm stock into the gelatin to dissolve. Gently stir the gelatin mixture and the vodka back into the stock. Chill the stock in the refrigerator overnight.

TO SERVE

Wash the celery stalk and use a potato peeler to cut it into thin strips. Wash the strawberries, remove the stems, and then cut them into slices. Arrange the rhubarb compote and the sliced strawberries in three bowls, then drizzle with some of the raspberry vodka stock. Garnish with a few strips of celery and a bit of rhubarb snow.

DARK BEER CHIBOUST, PUMPERNICKEL SAND & VINEGAR STRAWBERRIES

SERVES 3

INGREDIENTS

Pumpernickel sand
3½ oz/100 g pumpernickel bread
1 oz/30 g dark chocolate
2 tsp Grand Marnier

Vinegar strawberries
3 oz/90 g strawberries
¼ cup/50 ml apple juice
2½ tbsp sugar
2 tbsp apple cider vinegar

Dark beer chiboust
¾ tsp unflavored gelatin
7 oz/200 ml dark beer
1 large egg
3 tbsp sugar
2 tbsp wheat starch (or cornstarch)
2 tsp unsalted butter
Grated zest from ¼ organic orange
Salt

Other
Blender (such as a Vitamix Pro 750)

PREPARATION

Pumpernickel sand
1. Combine the pumpernickel, chocolate, and Grand Marnier in the blender jar and blend until finely ground. Cover and set aside until ready to serve.

Vinegar strawberries
1. Wash and stem the strawberries, then cut lengthwise into quarters. Mix the apple juice, sugar, and vinegar, then stir in the strawberries and refrigerate until ready to serve.

Dark beer chiboust
1. Soak the gelatin in ¼ cup/60 ml of the beer in a medium bowl to soften. Separate the egg, then whip the egg white and sugar until stiff.

2. In a saucepan, mix the egg yolk with the remaining beer, starch, butter, orange zest, and salt to taste. Heat the mixture, stirring constantly, until it thickens to a creamy consistency. Remove from the heat.

3. Stir the softened gelatin into the hot cream until dissolved. Gently fold in the meringue. Spoon the cream into three bowls and chill for 1 hour.

TO SERVE

Sprinkle the pumpernickel sand over the chiboust and top with the vinegar strawberries.

Bowl: studio1.berlin

PHYLLO-WRAPPED
BAKED APPLES

SERVES 3

INGREDIENTS

Filling
2 tbsp slivered almonds
4 oz/100 g marzipan
2 tbsp unsalted butter
1 large egg yolk
2 tbsp dried cranberries
2 tsp rum
Grated zest from ¼ organic orange
Salt

Baked apples
3 Braeburn apples
3 sheets phyllo dough

For serving
Powdered sugar

PREPARATION

Filling
1. Toast the slivered almonds in a skillet, then set aside.
   Knead together the marzipan and the butter. Mix in
   the egg yolk, cranberries, rum, orange zest, and salt
   to taste, then knead everything into a smooth dough.

Baked apples
1. Preheat the oven to 350°F/180°C and line a baking sheet
   with parchment paper. Wash the apples and scoop out
   the core. Stuff the apples with the marzipan dough.

2. Place the apples on the lined baking sheet and bake
   until tender, 25 to 30 minutes. Remove the apples
   and let them cool slightly. Increase the oven temperature
   to 410°F/210°C.

3. Spread one phyllo sheet out on your work surface
   and place one baked apple in the center of the sheet.
   Gently fold the phyllo dough up around the apple,
   wrapping it completely. Press the dough together firmly.
   Repeat with the remaining phyllo sheets and apples.

4. Set the wrapped apples back on the baking sheet
   and return them the oven for about 10 minutes,
   or until the phyllo dough is crispy.

TO SERVE

Set the phyllo-wrapped baked apples in three bowls
and dust with powdered sugar.

BIENENSTICH CREAM & ALMOND BRITTLE

SERVES 3

INGREDIENTS

Yeast cream
⅞ cup/200 ml heavy cream
7 tbsp milk
3 tbsp sugar
2 tbsp cornstarch
1 tbsp yeast
1 large egg yolk
2 tsp unsalted butter
2 tsp rum

Brioche croutons
2 oz/60 g brioche bread
2 tbsp vegetable oil
4 tsp unsalted butter
1 tsp sugar
½ tsp zest from organic orange
Ground cinnamon
Salt

Almond brittle
⅓ cup/50 g sliced almonds
2½ tbsp sugar
½ tsp unsalted butter
Salt

For serving
3 oz/90 g raspberries

PREPARATION

Yeast cream
1. In a saucepan, whisk together the cream, milk, sugar, cornstarch, yeast, egg yolk, butter, and rum.

2. Bring the mixture to a boil, stirring constantly, until it thickens to a creamy consistency. Pour the cream into a bowl, cover, and refrigerate until ready to serve.

Brioche croutons
1. Cut the brioche into large cubes. Heat the oil in a skillet and toast the cubes in the oil until golden.

2. Add the butter and sugar and gently shake the pan until the butter browns. Season the croutons with cinnamon and salt to taste and drain on paper towels.

Almond brittle
1. In a dry skillet, toast the sliced almonds until golden. While the almonds are toasting, add the sugar and 2 tablespoons of water to a pot, bring to a boil, and cook until the mixture is golden brown.

2. Add the toasted almonds, the butter, and a pinch of salt to the caramelized sugar mixture and stir. Spread out the brittle on parchment paper.

TO SERVE

Whisk the cold yeast cream until smooth. Wash the raspberries and pat dry. Place some of the raspberries and croutons in each of the three bowls and top with some of the yeast cream. Arrange the remaining berries and croutons on top of the cream, then garnish with the almond brittle.

BISCOTTI
& SWEET GUACAMOLE

SERVES 3

INGREDIENTS

Biscotti
1½ cups/190 g all-purpose flour
⅔ cup/135 g sugar
¼ tsp baking powder
2 medium eggs
4 tsp unsalted butter
⅔ cup/65 g pecans
⅓ cup/65 g almonds
Grated zest from ¼ organic orange
Salt, ground cinnamon

Sweet guacamole
1 large ripe avocado
½ banana
1 tbsp honey
1 tbsp lime juice
Grated zest from ½ organic lime
Red pepper flakes, salt

Other
Flour for work surface
Blender (such as a Vitamix Pro 750)

PREPARATION

Biscotti

1. Preheat the oven to 400°F/200°C and line a baking sheet with parchment paper. Combine the flour, sugar, baking powder, eggs, and butter and knead to form a smooth dough. Knead in the pecans, almonds, orange zest, and salt and cinnamon to taste.

2. On a floured work surface, form the dough into two logs about 15 inches/40 cm in length. Set the logs on the baking sheet and bake for about 15 minutes until golden brown.

3. Remove the logs from the oven and reduce the oven temperature to 350°F/180°C. Let the logs cool for 15 minutes, then use a serrated knife to cut them diagonally into slices about ¼ inch/6 mm thick.

4. Place the slices cut side down on the baking sheet and return them to the oven to toast for about 5 minutes.

Sweet guacamole

1. Slice the avocado in half and remove the pit. Scoop out the avocado flesh and weigh out 6 oz/175 g. Peel the banana and weigh out 2½ oz/70 g.

2. Combine the avocado, banana, honey, lime juice, lime zest, and pepper flakes and salt to taste in the blender jar and puree until creamy. Taste the guacamole and adjust the seasonings as needed.

TO SERVE

Divide the sweet guacamole into three bowls and serve with the warm biscotti.

Bowl: ASA

ABOUT US

BENJAMIN DONATH

Ben is a pastry chef, amateur photographer, and enthusiastic food blogger. Every week he publishes recipes on his blog, *EateryBerlin.com*. Along with the photos, the recipes entice his followers to try to replicate the dishes or simply spark their creativity. Ben works at a five-star hotel in Berlin, where every day he endeavors to inspire his guests anew. The success of the recipes in this cookbook can be attributed to Ben's background. His passion for food has become his profession. The desserts with their special flavors and varied textures carry his unmistakable touch. Born in Potsdam, Ben devotes himself to savory and sweet dishes in equal measure. His work in different kitchens and countries has truly expanded his horizons. For Ben, cooking is more than just a calling: In the kitchen, he is able to express his creativity, delight his guests, or simply leave the cares of everyday life behind. Ben always approaches ingredients with respect and dedication while taking care to enhance and not to lose their original character. His philosophy is to devote as much love and attention to the preparation of a simple dish as to a sophisticated multicourse meal. He loves the immediate feedback of watching the gestures and facial expressions of his guests from the moment they take their first bite. The highest possible praise for Ben are those small moments when guests' eyes catch sight of a dish for the first time and sparkle with excitement, when a guest's nose captures the first delicate hint of the spices, and when a guest guides the spoon to their mouth for the very first bite. It is this precise moment in which everyone recognizes whether a meal is delicious—no words are needed.

WWW.EATERYBERLIN.COM

VIOLA MOLZEN

Even when she was a young girl, Viola's favorite words were "the food is ready." She always associates places and trips with specific dishes: pizza at the Eiffel Tower, peppermint ice cream in Ireland, chorizo brioche in Lisbon, and pineapple pancakes in Vietnam. The list is long. So far the amateur chef has lived in the USA, the Netherlands, and Turkey, and currently she makes her home in Berlin. Yet Viola's love for food is evident in more than just her special gift for associating food with places. Viola's photos are confirmation enough: Whether as a child, teenager, or adult, nearly every photo shows the Lüneburg native eating. She recalls watching *Heidi* on TV as a girl and feeling jealous of the fresh goat milk and the delicious raclette cheese sandwiches that Heidi got to eat every day. Viola hums when she eats good food, and she has mastered the art of learning to love ingredients. If she doesn't like something, she continues to try it and eat it until it tastes good to her. Viola enjoys entertaining; she is a full-time connoisseur and loves to cook Turkish cuisine in particular—with plenty of cumin, cinnamon, and, most of all, lots of love.

ACKNOWLEDGMENTS

A project as wonderful as *Bowl Stories* could only become what it is today thanks in part to the generosity of the people and companies we had the pleasure of working with. We would like to express our gratitude for the loan of so many bowls and the fantastic equipment that made it possible for us to make many of these dishes in the first place. Furthermore, we would like to thank teNeues for the confidence they placed in us that allowed us to write this book—our first one. Without all of this support and without everyone who so generously helped us —unfortunately we are unable to list them all here—this book would not have been possible. We are thrilled, proud, and unbelievably happy.

We would like to extend special thanks to: 3PunktF, ASA, ferm Living, Royal Copenhagen, Staub / ZWILLING, studio1.berlin, and Vitamix.

INDEX

CASHEWS
Matcha Bircher Muesli 152
Miso Cream, Sake Pears & Cilantro
Streusel 142
CAULIFLOWER
Bowl with Wheat Berries & Tarragon
Croutons 14
Kale 10
Scallop Carpaccio, Cauliflower &
Raspberries 108
**Celeriac Pear Flan & Oven-Roasted
Onions 94**
CELERY
Beluga Lentil Salad & Sourdough
Bread 20
Raspberry Gazpacho & Olive Sticks 112
Rhubarb Bloody Mary Bowl 156
Roasted Potato Soup & Pickled Leeks 42
Sea Bass, Celery & Chili Strawberries 70
Chard Egg & Creamed Potatoes 56
Cherry Meringue 146
CHERRY JUICE
Berry Tapioca Pudding & Vanilla
Sauce 124
Cherry Meringue 146
Sour Cream Schmarrn & Blueberry
Pears 138
CHIA SEEDS
Guava Porridge & Grapefruit 122
CHICKEN
Coconut Chicken, Black Salsify
& Golden Oyster Mushrooms 72
Corn Cobbler 76
CHICKWEED
Asparagus Cappuccino 48
Coconut Chicken, Black Salsify
& Golden Oyster Mushrooms 72
**Chilled Cucumber Soup, Aloe Vera
& Kataifi 116**
**Chilled Pea Soup & Nectarine Yakitori
Skewers 90**
Chili Sin Carne 100
CHOCOLATE
Dark Beer Chiboust, Pumpernickel Sand
& Vinegar Strawberries 160
Egg Liqueur & Chocolate
Marshmallows 130
Mango Spring Rolls & Spiced Coffee
Dip 128
Miso Cream, Sake Pears & Cilantro
Streusel 142
Vanilla Pasta & Passion Fruit 150
Cobia Ceviche & Tamarillo Salad 102
COCONUT, SHREDDED
Cherry Meringue 146
**Coconut Chicken, Black Salsify
& Golden Oyster Mushrooms 72**

COCONUT MILK
Chilled Pea Soup & Nectarine Yakitori
Skewers 90
Coconut Chicken, Black Salsify
& Golden Oyster Mushrooms 72
Matcha Bircher Muesli 152
Scallop Carpaccio, Cauliflower
& Raspberries 108
Vegetable Curry & Couscous 44
COCONUT SUGAR
Cherry Meringue 146
Mango Spring Rolls & Spiced Coffee
Dip 128
Veal Tartare & Marinated Egg Yolk 12
COCONUT YOGURT
Matcha Bircher Muesli 152
Codfish Phô 46
COMTÉ
Œufs Cocotte 32
Corn Cobbler 76
CRANBERRIES, DRIED
Hokkaido Lasagna 16
Phyllo-Wrapped Baked Apples 162
CRÈME FRAÎCHE
Hokkaido Lasagna 16
Mango Spring Rolls & Spiced Coffee
Dip 128
Œufs Cocotte 32
Spiced Squash & Greek Frozen
Yogurt 134
**Crispy Chicken Liver, Rhubarb
& Mint Mashed Potatoes 82**
CUCUMBER
Chilled Cucumber Soup, Aloe Vera
& Kataifi 116
Matcha Bircher Muesli 152
Poached Salmon & Sorrel Stock 62
Raspberry Gazpacho & Olive Sticks 112
Salmon & Sake-Marinated
Cucumber 110
CURRANTS
Winter Roll 38
D
**Dark Beer Chiboust, Pumpernickel
Sand & Vinegar Strawberries 160**
DATES
Guava Porridge & Grapefruit 122
Radicchio Salad, Chorizo, Ricotta
& Dates 54
Dolma & Arugula Sauce 104
DUCK
Winter Roll 38
E
EDAMAME
Pear, Bean & Bacon 24
**Egg Liqueur & Chocolate
Marshmallows 130**

EGGPLANT
Chili Sin Carne 100
Vegetable Curry & Couscous 44
EGGS
Asian Carbonara 40
Asparagus Cappuccino 48
Asparagus & Passion Fruit Basil
Hollandaise Sauce 64
Asparagus Tempura & Shiso
Mayonnaise 78
Berry Tapioca Pudding & Vanilla
Sauce 124
Bienenstich Cream & Almond
Brittle 164
Biscotti & Sweet Guacamole 166
Celeriac Pear Flan & Oven-Roasted
Onions 94
Chard Egg & Creamed Potatoes 56
Cherry Meringue 146
Dark Beer Chiboust, Pumpernickel Sand
& Vinegar Strawberries 160
Egg Liqueur & Chocolate
Marshmallows 130
Heaven & Earth 26
Mango Spring Rolls & Spiced Coffee
Dip 128
Miso Cream, Sake Pears & Cilantro
Streusel 142
Œufs Cocotte 32
Pavlova, Salted Cream & Balsamic
Berries 140
Phyllo-Wrapped Baked Apples 162
Poppy Seed-Crusted Skrei & Kohlrabi 80
Salt-Crusted Beets 30
Sour Cream Schmarrn & Blueberry
Pears 138
Spiced French Toast 126
Veal Tartare & Marinated Egg Yolk 12
Wheat Beer Pretzel Bread Pudding 136
Wild Garlic Tagliatelle 88
F
FETA
Roasted Beets & Wild Garlic Pistachio
Pesto 98
FISH AND SEAFOOD
Cobia Ceviche & Tamarillo Salad 102
Codfish Phô 46
Mackerel, Onion Tapioca
& Sunchokes 106
Poached Salmon & Sorrel Stock 62
Prawns Flambé & Tomato Crostini 92
Salmon & Sake-Marinated
Cucumber 110
Scallop Carpaccio, Cauliflower
& Raspberries 108
Sea Bass, Celery & Chili Strawberries 70
Stuffed Calamaretti & Beefsteak
Tomato 66

IMPRINT

© 2016 teNeues Media GmbH & Co. KG, Kempen

Texts & photography by
Ben Donath & Viola Molzen
Design & layout by Sophie Franke
Translations by WeSwitch Languages,
Heather B. Bock & Romina Russo Lais
Copy editing by Cheryl Redmond
Editorial management by Regine Freyberg
Production by Nele Jansen
Imaging & proofing by David Burghardt/
db-photo.de

ISBN: 978-3-8327-3379-7
Library of Congress Control Number: 2016942248
Printed in Spain by Estellaprint

Published by teNeues Publishing Group

teNeues Media GmbH + Co. KG
Am Selder 37, 47906 Kempen, Germany
Phone: +49 (0)2152 916 0
Fax: +49 (0)2152 916 111
e-mail: books@teneues.com

Press department: Andrea Rehn
Phone: +49 (0)2152 916 202
e-mail: arehn@teneues.com

teNeues Publishing Company
7 West 18th Street, New York, NY 10011, USA
Phone: +1 212 627 9090
Fax: +1 212 627 9511

teNeues Publishing UK Ltd.
12 Ferndene Road, London SE24 0AQ, UK
Phone: +44 (0)20 3542 8997

teNeues France S.A.R.L.
39, rue des Billets, 18250 Henrichemont, France
Phone: +33 (0)2 48 26 93 48
Fax: +33 (0)1 70 72 34 82

www.teneues.com

ENJOY WITH teNeues

LIORA BELS
THE MIX
ISBN 978-3-8327-3381-0

JEAN-CHRISTIAN JURY
VEGAN CUISINE
ISBN 978-3-8327-3376-6

GRETHA SCHOLTZ
MATCHA – THE COOKBOOK
ISBN 978-3-8327-3399-5

LOHRALEE ASTOR & TALI SHINE
FEEDING THE FUTURE
ISBN 978-3-8327-3343-8

TALI SHINE & STEPH ADAMS
GOOD TO GLOW
ISBN 978-3-8327-3378-0

HRH PRINCESS TATIANA & DIANA FARR LOUIS
A TASTE OF GREECE
ISBN 978-3-8327-3337-7

ALPINE CUISINE
ISBN 978-3-8327-3401-5

LIVING OFF THE LAND
ISBN 978-3-8327-3424-4